WITH TOMORROW IN MIND

OCEANOGRAPHER
GENIUS
METEOROLOGIST
INVENTOR
CARTOGRAPHER
GEOPHYSICIST
SEAGRANT FOUNDER
RISKTAKER
COMIC STRIP WRITER
URBAN THEORIST
WILD CHILD

WITH TOMORROW IN MIND

How Athelstan Spilhaus Turned America Toward the Future

SHARON MOEN

UNIVERSITY
OF MINNESOTA

To MES for keeping it interesting
To Savanna and Sierra for keeping it real

and

To my Sea Grant colleagues—
Dr. Spilhaus would be so proud

© 2015 Regents of the University of Minnesota. All rights reserved.
The University of Minnesota is an equal opportunity educator and employer.

Produced by the University of Minnesota Sea Grant Program, Duluth, Minnesota.

ISBN 978-0-9965959-1-9
Library of Congress Control Number: 2015948518

The cover photo of Athelstan Spilhaus, circa 1958, is courtesy of the Dolph Briscoe
Center for American History, University of Texas at Austin.

Cover design: Russell Habermann, Minnesota Sea Grant
Page design: Zan Ceeley, Trio Bookworks
Editor: Mindy Keskinen

To order, contact:
Minnesota Sea Grant
31 West College St. Room 132
Duluth, MN 55812
email: seagr@d.umn.edu
phone: (218) 726-8106
www.seagrant.umn.edu

Unless otherwise noted, the information in this biography reflects Athelstan
Spilhaus's unpublished autobiography, *Spilly*, written with Joe Brown in the
mid-1970s, and Louise O'Connor's unpublished oral history *Athelstan Spilhaus:
A Man of Ideas*, compiled with Dr. Spilhaus's cooperation in the mid-1990s. Major
parts of these manuscripts are available at the Dolph Briscoe Center for American
History, University of Texas at Austin.

Printed in the United States of America

I'm impatient with the past and irritable with the present.
The future is where my concern lies
and I'm very optimistic about it.

—Athelstan Frederick Spilhaus

CONTENTS

FOREWORD

He might be called the ultimate Renaissance man. Athelstan Spilhaus's career encompassed achievements as an oceanographer, cartographer, meteorologist, inventor, sculptor, author, soldier, statesman, scientist, educator, advisor to presidents, and toy collector. As a creator who loved a challenge, he proudly declared that his career was an obvious exception to the popular notion that scientists today are overspecialized and out of touch. Indeed, many of his ideas on climate and oceans, environment and sustainability—even education and telecommunications—have proved to be highly relevant, even clairvoyant.

Never purporting to have answers for all the world's problems, he did suggest that he often knew what was wrong and how to approach the search for solutions. Spilhaus thought in terms of problems and sets of problems, devising logical and practical solutions to them. The new application of existing technology was one of his unique talents. In fact, after our years of friendship, I believe Athelstan Spilhaus was the greatest practical mind of our era.

We first met in 1977 when Dr. Spilhaus was a visiting scholar at the University of Texas at Austin Marine Science Institute. His second wife had recently died, and when not teaching, he seemed somewhat at loose ends. Consequently, a group of us spent many evenings visiting. It wasn't long before I realized his was no ordinary mind. Not only were Dr. Spilhaus's ruminations on current topics fascinating, his own life story was astonishing.

I began to think that someone should record his memoirs. That thought stuck with me over the next ten years. Each time our paths crossed, I realized anew that something important would be lost to future generations if his story was left unrecorded.

In 1987, when I was on the East Coast to conduct some interviews on another subject, I took a side trip to see Athel at his home in Middleburg, Virginia. The second day of our visit, I suggested that he should write an autobiography. He replied, "I can't write about myself."

Then, perhaps fortuitously, the weather intervened. A blizzard snowed us in for several days. Luckily, my tape recorder and camera were with me. We perused his extensive files, and I began to shape a manuscript that would document his astoundingly varied career.

I found a strong sense of self to be essential while working with Athel. As I continued working on the manuscript in the following years, interviewing many of his colleagues and friends, he constantly dared and challenged me to produce a work that he liked. He took his work and his play seriously without sacrificing his sense of humor. Dr. Spilhaus has been described as a cross between Falstaff and Einstein, and indeed, his sense of the absurd was one of his greatest charms.

He called things as he saw them without pandering to his audience's politics or personal views. Being with Athel was never boring, even when he was difficult—and he could, from time to time, be uniquely and originally difficult. When I accused him of that trait, he responded cheerfully, "The last time I was difficult was in 1946!"

Wherever he was, he was truly a catalyst, a "burr under the saddle blanket of the establishment," also variously described as a gadfly and a "Socrates given to the State by God." Noting his blend of scientific brilliance and social awareness, another observer said, "He feels that science or research must always have a purpose, even though that purpose may not be discovered until the research is complete." Many saw elements of true genius in him. And, although it is easy to associate genius with a driven personality, Athel belied that description. In fact, he was easygoing about almost everything but stupidity, mediocrity and unwillingness to learn.

In my estimation, Athel's greatest accomplishment was as an educator and teacher. Often, after a day with him, I found that I had gained a working knowledge of ideas that had seemed impossibly difficult before. He used clear language, easy for anyone to understand. His childlike glee when he invented something, no matter how simple; his pure joy in exploring the world; his ability to turn all topics into learning experiences—these were among his most endearing traits.

Athelstan had a way of changing every life he touched. Sublimely irreverent, his sense of humor could erupt at any moment on any subject, no matter how "serious." He was an amazing intellect. Whether you agreed with him on a subject was unimportant; his method of inquiry was fascinating, as was his delight in it. When I was with Athel, my mind seemed to work a little faster and more logically. Like so many others, I found him uplifting, challenging, and intellectually stimulating.

He also had some childlike qualities. During one of Athel's visits to my home, we took a break from a long interview session. In those few minutes, Athel decided to finish a project he had been working on and he needed a magnet for it. Noticing my refrigerator was covered with them, he proceeded to remove all but one for his project. Tearing the decorative housings off the magnets, he proclaimed them examples of "the absolutely idiotic trappings of modern society" as he gleefully finished his invention.

Although he often sparred with some of the world's top intellects, Athel was as interested in his own antique toy collection as he was in the major scientific discoveries and inventions of his day. He saw no contradiction there, either. He believed that all creative people should look at even commonplace objects and processes, and ask themselves if they can devise a way to do those things differently or better. Athel was a self-proclaimed child who never grew up. It takes a talent like his to pull this off and he did it with high originality.

His life and works offer us a unique and intimate look at the last century. Because he lived in interesting times, worked in interesting fields, and knew interesting people, readers of this biography will experience a cross-section of twentieth-century history through the inventions, eccentricities, and humor of a visionary who was deeply involved in many of its important events.

Athel was widely admired and sometimes disliked. However, in one way or another, he helped establish the norms of the era: he was a mentor to many people and the best company imaginable. He was an exceptional teacher, a steadfast friend if he decided he liked you—and an intellectual whirlwind. Whether you called him Spilly, Athel, or Athelstan—as I did on occasions when sternness was required—you were a better person for having known him.

Athelstan Spilhaus's papers now reside at the Dolph Briscoe Center for American History, University of Texas at Austin, where one can read his writings and marvel at his achievements.

I thank Athel for his cooperation. I also thank his late wife, Kathleen Fitzgerald Spilhaus, for being more than helpful. I must also thank her for her endless patience with my staff and me when we invaded her home and her files for days on end. I thank my former assistant, Paul Bardagjy, who is still covered in the dust from Athel's attic, Leah Glaze and Tommy Tijerina, my administrative assistants and mainstays, who sacrificed some lung capacity to the cause. To all who helped organize Athel and me and the mess we could create, thank you.

Louise S. O'Connor
Gaffney Ranch
Victoria County, Texas

Louise O'Connor in front of a sketch of Spilhaus's bathythermograph on the Wall of Discovery at the University of Minnesota Twin Cities, 2011.
Photo courtesy of Minnesota Sea Grant.

ACKNOWLEDGMENTS

D r. Stephen Bortone had an idea while serving as the director of the University of Minnesota Sea Grant Program. It was to have a biography of Athelstan Spilhaus written for history. Without Steve's and Sea Grant's support, the life of Athelstan Spilhaus might have remained beyond the reach of most people. I appreciated an oddly synergistic crossing of paths with Dr. Todd Wildermuth and our ensuing conversations as we pored over boxes of photographs, documents, video reels, and audio-tapes archived by Spilhaus's biographer, Louise O'Connor, at the Center for American History at the University of Texas at Austin.

O'Connor had tenaciously sintered down veritable mountains of information provided to her by Dr. Spilhaus and others into just under 500 pages of text, which informed my writing. Her gracious cooperation and unflagging belief that Dr. Spilhaus's life is worth examining both grounded and inspired this biography.

I thank the late Kathleen Fitzgerald Spilhaus for welcoming me into the Spilhaus compound in Middleburg, Virginia. I thank Joe Vadus and Cliff McLain, two of Dr. Spilhaus's closest friends, for their faith in my ability to relay "Spilly's story." Thanks, too, to Peter Elliott, Fred and Karl Spilhaus, and Claire Gace. I appreciate the tolerance of my assistants and daughters, Savanna and Sierra Moen. This biography is snappier and more fluid thanks to editorial suggestions from Dr. Michael Sierszen, John Steffl, Mindy Keskinen, and Konnie LeMay. My Sea Grant colleagues— Jeff Gunderson, Russell Habermann, Dee Angradi, Deborah Bowen—had a hand in this work, as did the staffs at the Dolph Briscoe Center for American History at the University of Texas at Austin and the Elmer L. Andersen Library at the University of Minnesota Twin Cities. This book came to fruition under the deft guidance of Beth Wright and Zan Ceeley of Trio Bookworks.

Truly, I am grateful for the assistance and enthusiasm that all of these people contributed.

TIMELINE

1911   Born, Cape Town, Union of South Africa, November 25

1922   Attends boarding school in England

1928   Builds "sand yacht" with Archie Elliott

1931   Earns B.S. in mechanical engineering, with honors, University of Cape Town

1933   Earns S.M. in aeronautical engineering, Massachusetts Institute of Technology (MIT)

1935   Files first patent: air condition indicator, April (issued February 1938)

       Weds Mary Atkins of Boston, June

1936   Becomes one of the first to drive from Cape Town to Cairo, with Mary

       Invents the bathythermograph as a research assistant at MIT/Woods Hole Oceanographic Institute

1937   Appointed chair of the meteorology department at New York University

1938   Files first patent for the bathythermograph, August (issued Oct. 1942)

First child is born (Athelstan Frederick Jr., or Fred)

1940   Second child is born (Mary Muir, or Molly)

1942   Third child is born (Eleanor, or Nellie)

1943   Becomes major in the U.S. Army through an Act of Congress

Fourth child is born (Margaret Ann, or Miannie)

1945   Tour of duty in North China

1946   Becomes a U.S. citizen

Awarded the Legion of Merit

Fifth child is born (Karl)

1947   High-altitude weather balloon launched by his project crashes near Roswell, New Mexico

Appointed by President Truman to assist the South African Meteorological Service

1948   Earns Ph.D. in oceanography, University of Cape Town

1949   Appointed dean of the Institute of Technology, University of Minnesota

1952   Awarded Exceptional Civilian Service medal, U.S. Air Force, Scientific Director of Weapons Effects

1954   Appointed by President Eisenhower to be the first U.S. representative to the executive board of the United Nations Educational, Scientific and Cultural Organization

1957   Begins authoring the *Our New Age* comic strips

1958   Satellite of the Sun is published, becomes popular, and is translated into other languages

1959   Received Patriotic Civilian Service Award from the U.S. Department of the Navy

1961   Appointed by President Kennedy to be U.S. commissioner to the Seattle World's Fair

1962   Introduces the idea of an experimental city

Awarded the Berzelius Medal from Sweden

Writes a daily comic panel during this year, in addition to the Sunday strip

1963   Introduces the idea of Sea Grant

1964   Divorces Mary

Weds Gail Thompson

1966   President Lyndon Johnson signs the National Sea Grant College Program Act, October 15

1967   Leaves the University of Minnesota to become president of the Franklin Institute

1969   Moves to Florida

1970   Appointed superintendent of the Palm Beach County School District to help desegregate a racially divided system, August 23

1971   Appointed as one of the first fellows of the Woodrow Wilson International Center for Scholars

Moves to Washington, DC

1972   With Gail, buys a home in Middleburg, Virginia

1973   *Sun Triangle* is placed in New York City

1974   Becomes special assistant to National Oceanic and Atmospheric Administration (NOAA) administrator Robert White

1978   Gail dies

1979   Marries Kathleen Fitzgerald

Becomes a serious mapmaker

Begins amassing a mechanical toy collection

1989   *Mechanical Toys: How Old Toys Work* by Athelstan and
Kathleen Spilhaus is published by Crown

1991   *Atlas of the World with Geophysical Boundaries Showing Oceans,
Continents and Tectonic Plates in Their Entirety* is published by
the American Philosophical Society

1998   Dies in Middleburg, Virginia, March 30

INTRODUCTION

SPILLY!

When broadcast journalist Walter Cronkite was asked to name the most interesting interviewee of his career, he replied, "Well, you may not have heard of him, but his name was Athelstan Spilhaus."
—**Cliff McLain**, aerospace engineer associated with NASA and humankind's ability to leave Earth's atmosphere

On September 12, 1963, teenagers sang along to *Surfin' Safari*, gasoline cost 29 cents a gallon, and people could watch one of three networks on black-and-white televisions. Americans were racing Russians to the moon. The nation was still jittery from the Cuban missile crisis, and within three months President Kennedy would be assassinated. On this day, a cabbie maneuvered through the streets of Minneapolis heading for the annual meeting of the American Fisheries Society. In the backseat was the keynote speaker, Athelstan Frederick Spilhaus, hastily tossing together the address he would deliver just minutes later. Likely, a blue haze surrounded the chain-smoking dean of the University of Minnesota's Institute of Technology.

By this time the South African–born Dr. Spilhaus was famous in scientific circles, primarily for inventing the bathythermograph, an instrument that revolutionized ocean research and became standard antisubmarine gear on Allied vessels during World War II.

1

He was an oceanographer, meteorologist, inventor, and forward thinker before the word "futurist" was commonly known. Spilhaus was also popular with the public. Ever the Renaissance man, he wrote a long-standing weekly syndicated comic strip, *Our New Age*, which entertainingly brought scientific ideas to Americans at their Sunday breakfast tables. He had also recently wowed the world with the science pavilion he organized for the Seattle World's Fair. By now a U.S. citizen, the ocean scientist was also annoyed with his adopted country for lagging behind many nations in fishing and other maritime activities. To Spilhaus, such mediocrity was intolerable.

That day in the taxi, Spilhaus contemplated ways to generate opportunities for more people to benefit from oceans and other waters. And having neglected to plan his speech beforehand, he was running out of time. Somewhere between the taxi and the podium, he formulated a challenge for the audience. Standing before his colleagues, he simply stated, "I think the time has come for sea-grant universities."

Astoundingly, in just three years and thirty-three days, these seminal words grew into the National Sea Grant College Program Act of 1966, modeled loosely after the Land-Grant College Act of 1862, which had funded many of the nation's agricultural schools. America's study of the oceans and coastal challenges would soon come of age.

Known affectionately as Spilly to some and Athel to others, the professor was adept at making impacts with both words and deeds. "When Athelstan Spilhaus had an idea, he had an audience," noted historian Todd Wildermuth.

In retrospect, Spilhaus's most important professional contributions to society were arguably the bathythermograph and the Sea Grant College Program. But, like an iceberg, the bulk of his innovations are less visible but even more impressive, partly in their sheer variety. At sixteen he invented what he called a "sand yacht" with his friend Archie Elliott. In his fifties he devised a "space clock" that displayed celestial information at a glance. He patented ice skates for the tropics, created the *Sun Triangle* sculpture in New York City, and is credited for initiating the pedestrian-friendly skyway systems now found in cities like Minneapolis. He ate with Mao Tse-Tung in northern China and drank with the future Pope Paul VI in Uruguay. He was a decorated World War II veteran who divorced one wife, buried another, and widowed a third. He fathered five children and held thirteen academic degrees.

By the time of his death on March 30, 1998, Spilhaus had written books on weather, the sea, social diversity, maps, and even mechanical toys (he was a serious collector, having amassed over 4,000 toys that needed no batteries or electrical cords). His numerous positions included an interlude as a school superintendent ensuring the peaceful integration of a racially divided district in Florida. Presidents tapped him for national service. A stint with the United Nations Educational, Scientific and Cultural Organization (UNESCO) opened his eyes to international diplomacy and helped earn him an unwanted spot on Senator Joseph McCarthy's "commie list."

Spilhaus was witty, if not always wise. Curious, if not always circumspect. Hubris gave him an edge, sometimes a serrated one. According to his FBI file, at least one peer considered him "a coarse bore." Some said Spilhaus, like a tumbling snowball gathering momentum and mass, tended to collect other people's ideas and, in a slightly changed form, absorb them as his own. He had a fondness for martinis and a sizable ego that required pampering by women, the public's attention, and the awe of peers. For a scientist, he had a rare flamboyance, but there is no doubt that he was fiercely talented and thrived under extreme pressure.

As his brother Muir put it, "The way Athelstan conducts himself, his general appearance and dress, his relaxations, his work and 'play,' the way he thinks and what he says and does, and even what he eats and drinks, his general demeanor—nothing is ordinary."

Athel fervently believed science *should* be a hobby for all and *could* be a career for some. He felt deeply that communicating science to the public and building interest in its potential was critical for the nation's continued success. He advocated for taking calculated risks as an American tradition, a key to the future.

Of course, any innovator has a share of mixed successes and even failures. Many of Spilhaus's early bathythermographs sank to the bottom of the ocean. Famously, one of his high-altitude weather balloons crashed in 1947 near Roswell, New Mexico, generating UFO hysteria and material for Hollywood and space-alien theorists to this day. The futuristic city he and a cohort of visionary friends and politicians created on paper in the 1960s never came to fruition, although it came tantalizingly close. Sea cities aren't thriving off the coast of Florida, as Spilhaus had pictured, and we aren't farming whales like cattle. But many of Spilhaus's visions *are* part of our world today: satellite communications, seawater desalinization, advanced aquaculture, and world map projections, to name just a few.

Spilhaus lived and worked against tumultuous backdrops including World War II, the dawn of space travel, the Cold War, and the social revolution of the 1960s. He pioneered remote data acquisition and sensing instruments for retrieving information from the sky and the ocean. He worked on ideas with notable contemporaries like futurist R. Buckminster Fuller, journalist Victor Cohn, politician Claiborne Pell, and oceanographer John Knauss. His closest friends included rocket scientists, ocean engineers, and ambassadors.

"Athel was a self-driven workaholic who became a basket case when he wasn't working," said Spilhaus's devoted third wife, Kathy. "He could not bear to deal with the details of everyday life and did not suffer fools gladly. . . . He couldn't stand to be idle or to see anyone else be idle."

If there were a sound track to accompany Spilhaus's adult life, it wouldn't be the Beach Boys' *Surfin' Safari*. More likely, the Boston Philharmonic would be slicing the air with Beethoven's Fifth Symphony, followed by Richard Strauss's *Also Sprach Zarathustra*, opus 30—the bracing theme music of the film *2001: A Space Odyssey*. The musicians would need all the bravado they could muster to keep up with the intense and unpredictable Dr. Spilhaus.

THE ORIGIN OF A FORCE, 1911–1931

Undoubtedly, I was difficult as a child.

—Athelstan Spilhaus

If Athelstan's childhood were set to music, it would be to the pulse of the songs being sung in the South African village of Ronde-bosch, where he was born on November 25, 1911. The fifth and last child of Karl and Nellie Spilhaus, impish Athelstan ran bare-foot through Rondebosch and over the fields of the farm until he was ten.

Of Spilhaus's childhood, one could call it irregular. It included visits from Rudyard Kipling, isolation, scholarship, and possibly a bolt of lightning. Whether the latter was fact or fiction, as he worked on his autobiography with Joe Brown, Spilhaus suggested that his earliest memories included being struck by lightning at the remote farm where his family lived during World War I.

His innate curiosity and creativity were nurtured by a bright mother, older sisters, and a series of English governesses. But maybe it was Athelstan's proximity to nature during boyhood that lured him down his multifaceted career path that blended science, art, policy, and engineering. By many accounts Athel spent an extraordinary amount of time out of doors compared to today's youth.

Baby Athelstan and his siblings, circa 1912. Photo courtesy of Kathy Spilhaus.

His brother Muir recounted that in boyhood Athel repeatedly exhibited an uncommon intelligence and a prankish nature. Indeed, his lifelong penchant for devilish fun might have been inherited. The surname Spilhaus is thought to be a shortened form of *Spielhausen*, German for "gambling house," which Athelstan later considered appropriate, or equally plausibly, "play your house away." Family lore holds that a card-playing ancestor had gambled away his entire wealth, including the family estate and house in Germany. His cousins paid the debt but required him to call himself *Spielhausen* as a solemn warning to his descendants. The family coat of arms still carries the six of hearts—the card on which the ancestral gambler evidently lost the family fortune.

Spilhaus's life, no doubt, took some of the turns it did because he had the good fortune of being born into a family that overtly valued intellectual and practical pursuits. Athelstan's parents set a sprightly pace toward an unconventional life, although their youngest son would later outdo them by far.

Karl Antonio (known as Carlos), Athelstan's father, was born in 1876 in Lisbon, and was orphaned at the tender age of two. His Portuguese mother died after giving birth to his sister Nita, who grew up to become a noteworthy painter of South African scenery. Not long after Nita was born, influenza swept across much of Europe, taking Carlos's father, a businessman, with it. Young Carlos grew up mostly under his grandfather's roof in Lübeck, Germany, mothered by an aunt and later by his grandfather's second wife.

As a youth Carlos served an apprenticeship with a shipping firm before he set off to seek his fortune in South Africa. At nineteen

Karl Antonio Spilhaus,
father of Athelstan Spilhaus,
circa 1950.
Photo courtesy of
Kathy Spilhaus.

he sailed from Hamburg across the world to join his great-uncle Arnold Wilhelm Spilhaus at the family firm in Cape Town.

"In the truest sense of the word, [he] was a merchant," Athelstan later said of his father. "He began his career buying scrawny sheep in the Kalahari Desert. He was thought to be the first white man to cross that desert."

Carlos found such success as a merchant that Jan Smuts, the prime minister of South Africa, appointed him European Trade Commissioner at the end of World War I. During the war, however, Carlos had been banished from Cape Town, as the government did not want a German citizen with shipping connections there. Leaving his family in Cape Town, Carlos moved to Johannesburg but found he was under constant surveillance. Unnerved, he decided it would be preferable to live within a P.O.W. internment camp instead. Carlos was eventually released on the condition that he and his family would live in a remote locale. This locale, Bellrock farm, became Athelstan's childhood playground. His two older brothers were at boarding school by this time, but four-year-old Athel, his parents, and his two sisters made a go of the farm life in the Imvani area, about 600 miles from Cape Town. They didn't really have an option, since Carlos's career in Cape Town had been abruptly halted at the outbreak of the war.

Speaking of his parents during that time at Bellrock, Athelstan said, "They didn't feel socially ostracized because they were physically ostracized. There wasn't opportunity to meet anyone to ostracize you."

Once the war ended, the Spilhauses returned from exile in the hinterlands to their home in Rondebosch—and also to business. Carlos invested in a share of a shipping agency, and, after his spell as trade commissioner in Europe, he became managing director of Cape Town's first cold storage firm. In Athelstan's opinion, "the Imperial Cold Storage Company grew into a hell of an outfit. He was shipping frozen mutton and hides to Europe."

Nellie Brown Muir
Spilhaus, mother of
Athelstan Spilhaus,
circa 1950. Photo
courtesy of Kathy
Spilhaus; adapted by
John Steffl.

Nellie, Athelstan's Scottish-born mother, had bragging rights
of her own. Born in 1878, she was the first woman to graduate
with a B.A. in math and physics from the University of the Cape
of Good Hope (now the University of South Africa). Possibly
she broke through this particular cultural barrier at the urging
of her father, Sir Thomas Muir, a famous Scottish mathematician and friend of Rudyard Kipling. The Muirs were lured from
Glasgow to South Africa when Nellie Brown was about fourteen. Diamond magnate Cecil Rhodes had become the sixth
prime minister of the Cape Colony and sought to reform the
education system there. He hired Muir as superintendent general of education.

Apparently in a eulogy, Lord Kelvin called Muir "the greatest
mathematician who ever lived." Reflecting on this, Athelstan commented, "I think that's a bit too much, myself . . . even if Kelvin did

say it. That is the difficulty with a biography, isn't it? Once a guy's dead, they say all kinds of nice things about him."

The Scottish grandfather Athelstan knew was rigid about many facets of life, particularly about the philandering of his youngest son, Thomas. Athelstan recalled, "[My grandfather] had a housekeeper named Miss Cogan, a dreadful person. She looked like a bloody dragon to me when I was a little kid. I suspect she was a sleep-in housekeeper. He was so tough on his son, but in his life he found it was necessary to have a companion. As a kid you wonder about these things."

Athelstan's life resonated with Muir's influence, his father's entrepreneurial spirit, and his mother's devotion to service. Athelstan admired his mother, not only for imparting her wisdom but

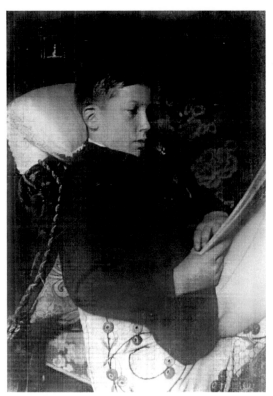

Young Athelstan engaged in one of his favorite pastimes, circa 1920. Photo courtesy of the Dolph Briscoe Center for American History, University of Texas at Austin.

also for teaching him her thrifty Scottish ways. He credited those habits as the source of the attitudes toward pollution and waste management that percolated through his later works.

"My mother had a remarkable career," he said. "After bringing up and educating five children, she was one of the first women in South Africa to enter politics. In the 1930s, she became the first woman member of the Provincial Council and devoted herself to the rights of women and colored people. Under Dutch Reformed Civil Law, married women had few rights. I always thought my mother was ahead of her time." The University of Cape Town awarded Nellie an honorary doctorate of law in 1955. Upon Nellie's death in 1973, Barbara Grieve, then president of the National Council of Women of South Africa, said, "If asked to give the names of the three most outstanding women South Africa has so far produced, I would include Nellie Spilhaus."

"I got a much better education at home," Spilhaus admitted. The positive learning of his formative years likely prompted his life-long interest in education, and not only his own. After he became a dean at the University of Minnesota, he inflamed teachers across the nation in 1957 by commenting at a press conference that high schools were teaching the three Ts (typewriting, tap dancing, and tomfoolery) rather than reading, writing, and arithmetic.

Athelstan recalls being lonely, but not solely because of isolation on the Bellrock farm. Not only was he the last sibling, but also a sister who would have been nearest to him in age died in infancy, before Athelstan was born. "I was naturally left out," Athelstan said. "My parents didn't intend it that way—it just happened. I was alone for much of my childhood with a very, very smart mother. I never went to school until I was ten. . . . Right up to MIT, I got honors in every damned thing I took, but it was lonely. I constantly built things and that got me into engineering."

Books and the equivalent of an erector set occupied the small boy. His sister Molly reported that at an impressively early age

Athelstan was reading aloud Rudyard Kipling's *Just So Stories* while the sisters sewed. He also disassembled old cars in the barnyard and played with the African and Afrikaner children with simple scavenged "toys."

Athelstan's oldest son, Fred, commented, "Dad is much more like his father than his mother. His father was very adventuresome and playful, and Dad has much of his bombast and ability to stretch the truth. They both have propensities to imbibe large quantities of alcohol. His mother was the smart one—very quiet and a strong disciplinarian. He got his standards for people and education from her."

"My parents didn't make the mistake of trying to handle me, which is a mistake often made," said Athelstan. "My parents were very busy and so they left me alone to grow up on my own. It was never through lack of love and I never felt unloved. Some might call my family controversial, but I call it advanced. Many members of my family on both sides have historically challenged the world around them, but always in a constructive way."

Molly recalled, "Athel made all the governesses' lives a misery. They never stayed longer than six months. Athel would do anything he could to irritate them. One time he was singing alternately one octave higher, then one octave lower than everyone else. The governess tried to cane him, and they both ran around the table faster and faster until Athel ran out the door, down the hill and into the river, where he stood laughing at the governess who couldn't get to him. He stripped off all his clothes and got naked. The governess was so shocked at the sight . . . that she screamed and ran off. We had a new governess shortly thereafter."

Athelstan's more traditional schooling began in England when the Spilhaus family relocated to Europe for three years in 1922. While his father conducted his trade commissioner's business out of The Hague to rebuild commerce interrupted by the war, Athelstan received a classical boarding school education—heavy on

Latin, Greek, French, English and mathematics—at Berkhampsted School in England.

He said, "I felt lucky to be in school. It was a privilege and still is. The problem in education today is that we have some stupid idea that everyone goes to school whether they want to or not; and therefore, they do not consider it a privilege. Either they feel the world owes it to them, or they go for the wrong reasons such as sports. There should be separate colleges for sports so as not to interfere with the athlete's professions by bothering to teach them to read and write."

Athelstan continued to feel a pervasive loneliness both at school, where colonials like him were viewed as fringe, and during school holidays, which he remembers spending in Holland with his father while his mother took his older siblings to Scotland. However, young Athelstan's holidays gave him an opportunity to cultivate a facility for languages and diplomacy.

After the family returned to South Africa, Athelstan finished out his high school days in Cape Town. Transitioning from high school to engineering coursework at the University of Cape Town, Athelstan captured the attention of the media for the first time at the green age of sixteen. He and Archie Elliott, his friend and eventual brother-in-law, had fabricated what was dubbed a "sand yacht" out of an automobile frame. A newspaper photograph showed young Athel sailing across salt flats on the contraption, foreshadowing a devotion to the sea and invention . . . and the press.

Along with dabbling in university high jinks and developing an appreciation for excellent teachers, Athelstan spent time during his mid-teens apprenticing with engineers on merchant ships. "I began at sea as an officer on the British ship *Luxme* of the Andrew Weir lines, based in Scotland," he recalled. "She was a vessel of opportunity that took coal from Natal [Brazil] and traded it for gunnysacks from Calcutta, as well as teak from Burma and other cargoes as

The sand yacht, circa 1928.
Photo courtesy of Peter
Elliott.

they came along. It was a great experience, although I doubt that it broadened my engineering knowledge. I did write a paper about maintaining diesels at sea and was very proud of it. It was my first publication and that is always a big thing."

Saltwater and sea shanties notwithstanding, Athelstan's interests lay in the air by the time he graduated in 1931 with a bachelor of science degree in mechanical engineering, with honors. At twenty, he was captivated by the aircraft business, which was just beginning to expand. Africa's vastness and its rudimentary road system suggested to him that air travel would make the continent more immediately accessible. And the air distance records that were being broken almost daily probably motivated the undeniable child in him to fly. Wishing to become an aircraft engineer and having a well-connected family, he wound up at the Junkers factory in

Germany helping to make some of the most innovative airplanes of that time.

"I don't know why I always chose to do things that were so far removed from friends and home," said Spilhaus. "It wasn't that I was antisocial, but I just seemed to choose these curious opportunities—rather lonely things to do—like working at sea with people who spoke a foreign language. And now, here I was in Germany." In the words of biographer Louise O'Connor, who knew him well, "He always wanted to do different things, as well as to do things differently."

A growing Nazi ideology in Germany quickly cooled the social climate and Athelstan's interest in being there. Athelstan decided to leave his volunteer apprenticeship and wend his way around Europe before making his way to the docks at Liverpool, where he took steerage passage on a steamship heading to America. "Steerage as a class wouldn't be around for very much longer," he said later. "You actually lived near the steering engine and ate very crude food. However, this didn't bother me. I found it interesting to experience the way immigrants came across to America many years before. So, off I went to America and my future."

Six months after leaving Junkers, a deepening interest in aerodynamics and a touch of wanderlust laced with naiveté had him knocking on a door at the Massachusetts Institute of Technology in Cambridge. What happened next is almost unimaginable in today's academic milieu.

Athelstan described the scene like this: "On arriving, I proceeded to dump my bags outside of Dean Lobdell's office. He was the dean of admissions. (This has become a famous story at MIT, or maybe they've forgotten it altogether! They used to tell me about it when I was on the corporation committees there.) It was getting on to the start of the term and I got in to see Dean Lobdell. First he said, 'Do you have an application in?' I replied, 'No, I wrote for a catalogue and just decided to come here.' 'You know,' he remarked,

looking me over, 'We get a lot of applications and we have to process them.' I said, 'Look, I've come all the way from South Africa.'
Dean Lobdell said, 'Well, did you go to school? Which college?' I
answered, 'University of Cape Town.' 'Never heard of it,' he said.
I'm reported to have replied, 'You will.'"

Despite the lack of an application backed by transcripts, rec-
ommendations, and test scores, Athelstan charmed the dean into
admitting him to the graduate program at MIT, on probation.
Spilhaus said, "After looking at MIT catalogues I decided to go
there, not even considering Caltech, because I didn't have enough
money to cross the U.S. . . . I think my mother liked the idea that I
was eager to study . . . but my father was not so keen on the whole
thing. He couldn't understand why I didn't come back to Africa
and go into business with him. Fortunately, my parents never tried
to choose my life for me to any great extent. Instead, they always
tried to help me make my own decisions."

2

LOVE AND WAR, 1932–1948

The story of their . . . trip . . . would make science fiction
look commonplace. —**Robert Abel**, founding director of the
National Sea Grant College Program, on the Cape to Cairo adventure

Spilhaus's drive and intelligence were abundant, but they weren't enough to put him through graduate school at MIT. He needed money. In the end, whiskey helped finance his master's of science degree in aeronautical engineering.

Ironically, Spilhaus needed a boat to pay for his studies of flight. Along with some university mates, Spilhaus gathered cases of scotch and other whiskeys that had been pitched into the ocean off Cape Cod. The boys rounded up the valuable flotsam and sailed the illegal cargo to a beach as retrievers in a rum-running trade that developed during Prohibition.

"We never saw who picked them up," he said. "We were a little ambivalent about the repeal of Prohibition, but this operation certainly helped me get through MIT."

Legitimate money came by way of the air mass indicator (aka air condition indicator), which was a device that simultaneously measured relative humidity and temperature. Spilhaus's first patented invention

Athelstan Spilhaus as a
young man, circa 1930.
Photo courtesy of the Dolph
Briscoe Center for American
History, University of Texas
at Austin.

merged two tools already popular among meteorologists: a thermom-
eter made with a temperature-sensitive coil and a hair hygrometer
for measuring humidity. With these gauges, the device provided a
reasoned commentary on how comfortable a room might feel. Was
it muggy or dry? Raw or keen? Now you could really know. A 1935
issue of *Popular Science* referred to the device as a "comfortmeter."

"It transformed something as ethereal and misty as the atmosphere into something measurable to the rational mind," Wildermuth wrote. "The comfortmeter pulled the atmosphere out of the
ether . . . what had before been only air was now data."

An air conditioning company purchased the rights of
Spilhaus's comfortmeter, and it "was the last anyone heard of my
invention," said Spilhaus. Or so he thought. Today you can purchase a comfortmeter, a device derivative of Spilhaus's design,
for about $90.

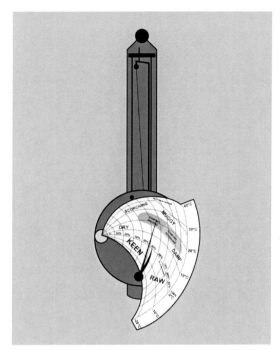

The air mass indicator, Spilhaus's first patented invention. Illustration by Russell Habermann, Minnesota Sea Grant.

Later in his life, Spilhaus would say, "There is no true invention. It is the synthesis of dissimilar things in the mind that leads to invention. It is only taking old ideas and combining them for new purposes." The air mass indicator was an early testament to this sentiment.

Spilhaus relished the intellectual challenge of studying at MIT and felt so inspired by its professors that he recalled, "Before long I wasn't just studying—I was working like a dog." (He was also acting, playing "the Englishman" in at least one production staged by the MIT dramatics society.)

Fortuitously, Spilhaus shared an apartment with Charles Stark Draper, a man who went on to invent a guidance system that made possible the Apollo space program and Neil Armstrong's "one small step for [a] man, one giant leap for mankind." Draper coauthored one of his first manuscripts on gyroscopes with Spilhaus, and Spilhaus credits Draper with being one of the greatest influences in his life.

"I was sort of a young playboy, but Stark kept disciplined hours," Spilhaus said. "When you roomed with such a fellow, you studied, too. . . . I really got excited about being a student at MIT and worked very hard."

After earning a master's degree in aeronautical engineering, meteorology became Spilhaus's next academic pursuit thanks to the subject's riveting instructors. While still at MIT as a research assistant, he realized that understanding airflow didn't mean that humans had mastered the air. Aircrafts were especially affected by the weather's whims. Since Spilhaus believed that good engineering considers both the medium and the machine, he sought to learn as much as he could about weather patterns for the next several years.

During those same several years Athel courted Mary Atkins, a Vassar graduate. Mary was a member of the distinguished Bostonian Hornblower family by way of her mother, Ruth. Mary's father, Robert Wrisley Atkins, was born into a family whose interests and fortune were deeply rooted in the Cuban sugar trade; he joined the family firm E. Atkins & Co., but also became involved with real estate, banking, and other pursuits over his lifetime.

Mary was also the granddaughter to the aged friend that inspired Athel to invent the air mass indicator. Mary's conservative and impeccable upbringing likely left her vulnerable to Athel's roguish charm and adventurous spirit. The couple married in Cuba in June 1935.

Goddaughter and niece, Claire Gace, remembers Mary as akin to a fairy godmother. "When Aunt Mary and Uncle Athel would fly over to visit us in South Africa, she would always bring me a charm for my bracelet and the newest Newbery Award-winning book," she said. "She was beautiful and utterly true. Granny [Nellie Spilhaus] adored her. She thought Mary was absolutely sterling." Indeed, the friendship between Mary and Athel's mother lasted for the duration of their lives, as did Mary's affection for all of her South African relations, including Athelstan. After marrying and moving to the U.S., Gace and her family often summered in Cape Cod with Mary, long after her divorce from Athel. "Mary was an accomplished spring-board diver and pianist," said Gace. "For a woman who was raised so terribly carefully, she approached life, including the dramatic societal changes it encompassed, with impressive generosity and grace."

Soon after Athel and Mary were wed, Athel whisked his new bride to South Africa for a year that included his military stint as a temporary first lieutenant destroying dud artillery shells left over from the Boer War. His rank and his assignment as assistant director of technical services in the South African Defense Force also gave him access to airplanes.

"The old colonel in charge gave me a lot of freedom and the available airplanes weren't being used for any warlike plans, so we could use them for other purposes," he recalled. "The airplanes were biplanes with enough string between the wings so that you could put a canary in it that could never get out. . . . I started the first routine upper air ascents to make meteorological measurements in the southern hemisphere. We went up without oxygen to about 16,000 feet in open cockpit biplanes. We'd try to get to 18,000 feet with our little meteorograph attached to the wing. When we began to black out, we would dive to breathe. I got the first records in the southern hemisphere like that."

As much fun as blacking out at high altitudes must have been, Spilhaus missed the stimulation of academia, especially the caliber of science being pursued at MIT. He cabled one of his old professors, who arranged a position for Athelstan with funding from Woods Hole Oceanographic Institution. Though eager to start his new job, Athel was equally eager to make an adventure of the trip back to the States.

Athel and Mary's exodus from Africa began with a 1933 Buick Roadster, a compass, and an ambitious scheme to drive from

Cape Town, South Africa, to Alexandria, Egypt. Although the Spilhauses were among the earliest people to navigate the length of Africa in a vehicle, they weren't the first to try. Boer War veteran Captain R. N. Kelsey began an attempt in 1913 that came to an abrupt end when he was mauled by a leopard and subsequently died of gangrene. The first completed and recorded journey from Cape Town to Cairo occurred in 1924, when Major Chaplin Court Treatt's expedition drove the distance in two light trucks.

The young Spilhaus duo, though, deserves enormous credit for proving that civilian adventurers could also make the journey. En route they meticulously documented their altitude with an aneroid altimeter, along with the curious experiences unique to the nearly roadless Africa of 1936. Sometimes navigating with only a compass and a view of the horizon, Athelstan said it was like sailing a boat. Their fascinating and harrowing trip diary can be found at the Dolph Briscoe Center for American History at the University of Texas at Austin as is *Cape to Cairo*, a 1990 documentary film in which a gray and balding Athelstan recounts this youthful adven-

Friend Archie Elliott (left) with Athelstan, Mary, and the Roadster in 1936.
Photo courtesy of Peter Elliott.

Alexandria
Cairo
Great Temple of
Abu Simbel

Mangbetu
Tribe→

Mt. Kilimanjaro

SPILHAUSES' TRIP THROUGH
AFRICA   Cape Town

Map of the Spilhauses' Cape-to-Cairo drive.
Map by Russell Habermann, Minnesota Sea Grant.

ture. The *Cape to Cairo* documentary by Louise O'Connor can also be viewed on the Minnesota Sea Grant website: www.seagrant. umn.edu/about/spilhaus.

Ranging from marketplaces to mountaintops, the couple dared a difficult, dangerous, and singular journey covering well over 5,000 miles of rugged terrain. More than fifty years later Athelstan still vividly recalled how members of a Pygmy tribe near the Rwenzori Mountains helped free the couple's mud-stuck convertible with a brand of culturally unique hilarity and disorganization. During the mostly off-road "road trip," Athelstan noted how the pitch of rooflines changed in relation to wind and rain patterns.

These observations surfaced multiple times in his later writings about societies and city design.

The trip took nine weeks and claimed all the springs in the Roadster. It led them beside the "grey-green, greasy Limpopo River" immortalized by Rudyard Kipling. It led them to the Mangbetu tribe, to merchants selling human flesh, and past the Great Temple of Abu Simbel in its original locale (it was relocated under the UNESCO Nubia Campaign in 1968). Finally arriving at the coast in Alexandria, the Spilhauses loaded their Roadster and themselves aboard a ship and headed for the United States.

Necessity and Invention

Spilhaus is so weary of the ballyhoo that has followed this 1930s invention that he tries never to talk about it; however, it follows him—haunts him—for the simple reason that it genuinely revolutionized oceanography. —**Cheryl Wetzstein**
in a 1986 article, "Athelstan Spilhaus: Ideas, Ideas, Ideas"

Spilhaus reentered the world of research through the door opened by Dr. Carl-Gustaf Arvid Rossby, a brilliant mathematical physicist, meteorology pioneer, and unusual character in his own right. Bridging a thirteen-year age difference, Spilhaus and Rossby had notable similarities. Both were foreign nationals (Rossby was Swedish). Both were convinced that understanding weather required grasping the interactions between the atmosphere and the oceans. Both had enormous energy and enthusiasm for their subjects and "a Hollywoodian flair for dramatic executive actions."

Rossby was the first person to describe the mechanics of winds and their meanders in the upper atmosphere. He was also a person who recognized Athelstan Spilhaus's potential, or, as many would call it, genius.

Soon after returning to Massachusetts in 1936, Spilhaus found new ways to combine his aerospace interests and mechanical engineering skills. As a research assistant connected with Rossby's work at MIT and Woods Hole Oceanographic Institution, he patented an improved gyroscope and an in-flight calculator that let pilots quickly measure the distance between themselves and objects in their vertical airspace, even diffuse objects such as clouds. But his biggest coup was the bathythermograph. He said, "I spent the academic year 1936–1937 at MIT. That was the year in which I invented several funny things in my spare time and the bathythermograph was one of them."

This instrument for collecting data from the ocean was inspired by Rossby's quest to understand eddies in the Gulf Stream.

Oceans are not homogenous—they are not like a gallon of homogenized milk; they are frequently layered, like a vinaigrette salad dressing. Rossby sought to describe the workings of a stratified ocean, where a warm layer of water lies above a denser, colder layer. He wanted to understand how wind and currents shunted warm Gulf Stream water toward the Massachusetts coast. Realizing that they couldn't properly study eddies without a rapid way to measure temperature, Rossby challenged Spilhaus to invent the appropriate tools.

Applying his knowledge of air currents, Spilhaus began by designing a way to simulate ocean currents. For the experiments he wanted to conduct, he needed space for a giant rotating basin of water. That is how and when the men's bathroom in the cellar of MIT's mechanical engineering building came to be his laboratory. "These were not the plush days of research—we just did with what we had. I was delighted to get it, as the power, plumbing and drains were all in," he said. "The amusing thing about these experiments was that people would wander into this men's room and think the giant dishpan was some fancy new kind of urinal!"

Spilhaus described this "dishpan" as "a six-foot shallow cylinder on a very thick steel bed, running on three rubber wheels, rotating in the manner of the Earth from the northern hemisphere." Water jetted out of a small slit at the center of the pan, and Spilhaus photographed the resulting patterns of flow. After detecting eddies, he realized that he couldn't really measure them in the ocean without a rapid temperature-measuring instrument. A basement bathroom seems a more likely place to be conducting experiments with mold and cockroaches, but this is where he conceived the bathythermograph—an instrument that would become a consequential tool for research as well as war.

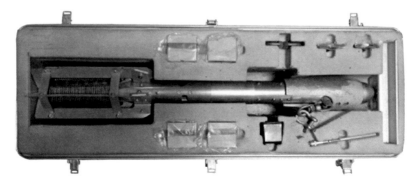

The bathythermograph, also known as the BT. Photo by Sharon Moen. Minnesota Sea Grant.

The bathythermograph, or BT, was a tool that could reveal the temperature-pressure profile of the ocean. The torpedo-shaped instrument was about as long as a baseball bat and as heavy as a pickaxe. A sailor could lower a BT into the ocean on a long wire while the ship was underway. As the BT sank, the increasing pressure of water gradually compressed the metal bellows housed at the tail end of the casing. As the bellows moved, they pulled a glass microscope slide smoked with skunk oil with them. At the front end of the BT, a strip made of two metals controlled a stylus that drew on the glass slide. The two metals contracted at different rates making the bi-metal strip bend according to changes in water temperature. Thus the stylus inscribed the strip's response to temperature over the smoked slide, which was moving according to pressure. In short, the characteristics of the water initiated motion within the BT that placed a line graph on the slide, with the vertical axis showing pressure (a proxy for depth), the horizontal axis recording temperature.

Spilhaus published his first public description of his design for the bathythermograph in 1938 and concurrently filed a patent for it. It was the first device to continuously record both temperature and pressure as it descended through the ocean to depths of 150 meters. "It rendered water more legible to the rational mind," in Wildermuth's words. Like the comfortmeter, this device displayed the relationship of two variables.

Three patents and a stack of professional publications later, Spilhaus and Rossby had used the BT to describe ocean secrets such as vertical temperature structures, lateral mixing, and large eddies at the edge of the Gulf Stream. But something important happened before the BT was fully developed.

While Spilhaus was experimenting with bathythermograph prototypes (and losing quite a few to Davy Jones's locker in the process), the U.S. Navy approached Dr. Columbus Iselin, one of his supervisors and the associate director of Woods Hole Oceanographic Institution. It was 1937, and the navy had a problem: its engineers were mystified by the erratic reliability of their sonar systems. These were the early days of "sound navigation and ranging," or sonar. After missing target after submarine target, the naval engineers suspected their problems were caused by some unknown variable in the water itself, not in the equipment. Much to the military's initial consternation, Spilhaus—still a British citizen thanks to his South African heritage—joined Iselin on an excursion to the navy's secret test site in Guantanamo Bay, Cuba.

Working alongside the crew of the research vessel Atlantis in August 1937, Spilhaus recalled, "We were trying to convince them that it was the thermal layering of the oceans and the lens-like bending of the sound waves by the thermocline that were responsible for the misses."

Using an early model of the BT, Iselin discovered a new and important ocean phenomenon—the "afternoon effect." The BT enabled them to document the extent to which the afternoon sun heats the top ten meters of surface water, in effect, making "time of day" a variable in the sonar equation. Together with existing knowledge of temperature, depth, and salinity as factors, this new understanding allowed navy personnel to adjust weapon trajectories and more accurately target enemy submarines.

Spilhaus's renown was growing. Toward the end of 1937, still a mere twenty-six years old, he was recruited from his lavatory laboratory to found and chair the meteorology department at New York University (NYU). Spilhaus soon became one of the youngest faculty members to be given a full professorship at a major university, earning it with a brash and innovative approach to weather forecasting. With balloons, flares, and cameras, he monitored the skies and captured the attention of the media. By 1938 he had developed his own methods of charting night winds and was showing off his inventions to the American Meteorological Society. But what gave Spilhaus arguably the greatest satisfaction was the day Raymond Montgomery, a theoretical oceanographer, joined the department at NYU. "I believed the weather couldn't be understood without studying the ocean," Spilhaus said. "I felt that one shouldn't have a department just for meteorology without attacking oceanography."

To a rare extent, Spilhaus combined intellectual prowess with practical observation of nature. Todd Wildermuth observed in his dissertation, *Yesterday's City of Tomorrow: The Minnesota Experimental City and Green Urbanism*, that Spilhaus's earliest writings were particularly focused on what might be called "proper" science:

In [his earlier writings], Spilhaus described natural phenomena in formal terms: wind vectors, ground friction and eddy viscosity. He spoke the language of pure Newtonian lag equations and logarithmic expression, azimuths and hair hygrometers. In person, however, Spilhaus lived the young man's dream of working under the sun. His science was directly connected to nature, and nature was part of his life.

He detected unseen or not easily seen natural phenomena and seemed to take pleasure in doing so, perhaps because he was so good at it. He detected wind patterns in the upper atmosphere of South Africa. He probed the temperature profile of the oceanic Gulf Stream. He described the ozone content of New York City air. Wherever life put him, it seems, Spilhaus tried to measure or detect some component of his physical surroundings, aided always by some device that extended his senses. When the device did not exist, he would set out to invent one.

Apparently, scientific instruments spilled into the Spilhaus home, too. Of his boyhood, Mary and Athel's first son, Athelstan Frederick Jr. (Fred), recalled, "Our toys were often broken scientific equipment. He was unconsciously trying to teach us all the time." Fred was born in 1938. Four more children followed: Mary Muir (Molly) in 1940, Eleanor (Nellie) in 1942, Margaret Ann (Miannie) in 1943, and Karl in 1946. Later, Fred recalled that their father involved all of them in scientific tinkering, even if it meant they were refilling his bourbon glass or fetching him a pair of pliers.

But Fred was still an infant in 1939, when Hitler began his attempt to rule Europe and beyond. World War II sent practically every person, enterprise, and industry into a tailspin. Spilhaus and the NYU research units were no exception. Scientific energy from academic, private, and government sectors was now channeled toward supporting the Allied forces. For Spilhaus, the focus became forecasting the weather for military strategists.

Meanwhile, even before the United States entered the war, British brass asked President Roosevelt for 200 bathythermographs for their ships. Too many of the Royal Navy's destroyers were being sunk at the entrance to the Strait of Gibraltar, where German submarines, those menacing U-boats, were evading the destroyers' sonar. The Germans understood that the less-saline water from the Mediterranean floated out of the Strait atop the saltier Atlantic water flowing in underneath. The density difference between the layers acted as a mirror to a sonar ping sent out by a destroyer. German subs escaped detection if they stayed below the abrupt density change. Britain hoped that the bathythermographs would help the Allies' navies discern the conditions and depths in which enemy subs might be lurking and, in turn, lurk there themselves.

Spilhaus gave the U.S. military permission to manufacture the BTs. Woods Hole professor Maurice Ewing and his student, Allyn Vine, helped perfect the instrument, and soon the Submarine Signal Company was manufacturing it in quantity. BTs became standard equipment on antisubmarine warfare (ASW) watercraft and were particularly useful in Mediterranean and Japanese waters, where temperature gradients were the most troublesome.

As Athelstan later recounted, "The United States went into the mass production of BTs and put them on every destroyer. During the defensive stage of the war, when the Germans were harassing our destroyers and convoys, the main purpose of the bathythermograph was for evasion purposes. Once the tide of war turned, our antisubmarine forces used the BT on the offensive. Apparently, the Germans never found out about it. The BT was classified top secret, of course, which was rather pointless since I had invented it in peacetime. That is one of the funny things about science."

After the war, Winston Churchill wrote Spilhaus a personal thank-you letter for his oceanographic contribution to the Allies' victory. Over fifty years later, at Spilhaus's funeral in 1998, Robert Abel, founding director of the National Sea Grant Program, noted,

Athelstan Spilhaus served in
the U.S. Army during World
War II, despite being a citizen of
the Union of South Africa, 1945.
Photo courtesy of Kathy Spilhaus.

"The importance of this invention to modern naval warfare cannot be understated." Moreover, the bathythermograph lifted oceanography out of the expedition stage of observation and into a synoptic stage, where data could be gathered in a way to construct a larger description of the physical ocean. It was the first oceanographic instrument with which researchers could get an almost "real-time" picture of oceanic conditions.

While the Allies reaped the military benefits of the BT in the early 1940s, Spilhaus was conducting weather-related operations for the U.S. Army Air Corps. Still a citizen of the Union of South Africa, he joined the U.S. military in 1943 thanks to a special, wartime act of Congress. As Athelstan said later, "I was young and able-bodied and the only place for me was at war."

For the next two years Major Spilhaus (later to become Lieutenant Colonel Spilhaus) coordinated the research and development of meteorological equipment. The five-foot-eight, 180-pound major did this primarily, but not exclusively, from a laboratory in

New Jersey. Toward the end of the war, Spilhaus could be found behind Japanese enemy lines establishing covert weather stations and reporting weather to U.S. bombers flying out of Guam and Saipan. The man drawing those enemy lines was Mao Tse-Tung (Zedong), soon to be chairman of the People's Republic of China. At that time Mao was leading the Chinese Communist resistance against the Japanese in the Second Sino-Japanese War, which had merged with World War II. In 1945, serving as coordinator of research of army weather equipment, Spilhaus lived in a cave in Yenan, North China, a stone's throw from the cave occupied by Mao.

"Mao was the big shot and I was just a young major with a job to do at his headquarters; but I did see him a number of times," Spilhaus recounted later. "My job depended on his good wishes and the help his troops could offer. . . . The picture I carry with me of those days is a simple one. It is evidence of the strength and discipline that only those who were there at the time saw so clearly. Discipline and strength were the underlying factors in Mao's

Athelstan (middle) coordinated the research of army weather equipment during World War II. Photo courtesy of the Dolph Briscoe Center for American History, University of Texas at Austin.

remolding of the new China we see today. . . . If I painted a sympathetic picture of Mao it was because I really believed he was a great world leader."

In the notes of a speech, later found in his papers, Athel gives two reasons for respecting Mao: the Chinese leader insisted on stringent health laws, and he practiced recycling. Spilhaus also observed, "As in any theater, including a theater of war, your view of the scene as the curtains begin to part depends on where you sit. In North China, I had a box seat." This is maybe why Spilhaus's sympathies lay with Mao and why he found Roosevelt's domestic policies and Chiang Kai-shek's leadership contemptible. For Spilhaus's wartime contributions, Chiang Kai-shek's army put a $20,000 dead-or-alive bounty on his head, and the U.S. Army pinned a Legion of Merit medal on his chest.

Athelstan returned to civilian life somewhat reluctantly, just before Christmas 1946. He had made quite a name for himself with his combat exploits and his wartime accomplishments, both scientific and diplomatic. One of Spilhaus's first acts upon stepping on American soil again was to become a U.S. citizen. Spilhaus said, "I was in uniform, a Lieutenant Colonel with a lot of decorations. . . . I asked Colonel Marcellus Duffy and a colleague, Major John Peterson, to be witnesses for me at Columbus Circle when I took the oath of American citizenship. I hadn't passed any exams or anything, but I had to become a citizen because I knew too damn much to get out of uniform. I think it would have been awkward if I had remained a British subject. I had no objections to becoming an American now that the war was over."

Spilhaus didn't realize how important the bathythermograph had become until he returned from his overseas military duties. After fulfilling Britain's request, the United States had been mass-producing BTs for its own destroyers as well.

When Spilhaus developed the BT some eight years earlier, he imagined rightly that it would become a standard instrument for ocean research. He had approached MIT senior faculty member Jerome Hunsaker, thinking that the University would want to patent it. After taking the idea to the MIT patent committee and considering the very few people working in ocean science at the time, Hunsaker wrote Spilhaus a letter saying, "We agree every oceanographer will want one, all six of them. . . . You keep the patent. MIT has no interest."

Now, when the professor returned from his post in China and Army Air Corps duties, he "found that nearly every damn ship had one of [his] devices on it." Since thousands had been manufactured during World War II, Spilhaus's patent was now valuable. Wishing to profit financially from his invention, he hit the navy up for royalties as the inventor, a U.S. citizen, and a veteran of war.

"This was one time I deliberately put on my uniform," he recalled. "I put on every darned bit of brass I could hang on—the leaves of a Lieutenant Colonel, gongs and little headquarters stars, hash marks, everything. The only time I've ever done it, not counting when I took the oath of citizenship. I went down to the navy and saw their lawyers and we negotiated the matter. I think they were a little hesitant to be tough with a guy who'd been overseas."

The navy, indeed, paid Spilhaus his royalties, enough for him to feel that he had extra money for the first time in his adult life. With his surplus he built a house on Cape Cod: close to Woods Hole for summer pursuits on the sea and near enough to NYU, where he had stepped back into his professorship.

At NYU, Spilhaus served on advisory committees, recruited and groomed talent for the university, and continued his work of linking universities and government in research efforts. As a member of the Committee on Geophysical Sciences of the Joint Research and Development Board, he helped coordinate the interests of the War and Navy Departments to help align research goals with national defense. Indeed, by 1947, Americans were exhibiting a new enthusiasm for applied science—and a palpable fear of the Soviet Union.

Eyes on the Skies

It would be unfair to blame Athelstan Spilhaus for what
came to be called the Roswell Incident. All the same, he was
the engineer in charge of an experiment that resulted in many
otherwise sane people becoming convinced that aliens
had arrived on earth. —*The Economist*, 1998

At NYU, Spilhaus and his colleagues were now investigating ways
to fly balloons across the Atlantic. "The Japanese had flown fire
balloons from the Japanese Islands to the Oregon forests and we
were emulating these balloons, thinking we might use them for
meteorological purposes," he said. "The prevailing winds were
west to east and we succeeded in having controlled altitude balloons that landed in Europe."

Now in his mid-30s, Spilhaus was soon involved with a variety
of curious balloon projects, one of which begat enough fodder for
UFO enthusiasts to still be chewing on more than six decades later.
The name "Roswell Incident" has become synonymous with alien
spacecraft in many a fertile mind. In reality, the mysterious airborne
debris found by a rancher in New Mexico was the remains of a highly
classified high-altitude balloon experiment involving the NYU Balloon Group, of which Spilhaus was a leading member—although
the group wasn't fully aware of the applications of their own work.

In fact, the NYU Balloon Group was contributing to what was
later revealed as the top secret Project Mogul. With the world's
political temperature chilled to a cold war, the U.S. government
was trying to track the Soviets' atomic weapons testing. As there
were no satellites at this point in history, NYU's balloons were to
monitor the skies for evidence. Carrying equipment to detect sound
waves generated by Soviet nuclear detonations and the acoustical
signatures of ballistic missiles, the balloons were to traverse the
upper atmosphere at a steady altitude.

Project Mogul was inspired by one of the scientists involved with perfecting Spilhaus's bathythermograph, Maurice Ewing. While conducting research for the navy during World War II, Ewing, a professor at Woods Hole, proved that explosions could be heard thousands of miles away with underwater microphones placed at the ocean depth known as the "sound channel." Ewing theorized that a region in the upper atmosphere might conduct sound in a similar way.

Project Mogul focused on developing three areas of technology: (1) an expendable microphone, capable of detecting long-range, low-frequency sounds generated by explosions and missiles; (2) a means of delivering these sounds to a ground or airborne receiver; and (3) a system from which to suspend hardware in the upper atmosphere for an extended time. To meet the first two goals, contracts for the acoustical equipment were awarded to Columbia University, where Ewing then worked. NYU won the contract for the third item: the constant-level balloons.

With Spilhaus as director of research, the NYU group made three trips to Alamogordo Army Air Field during the spring and summer of 1947 to test and evaluate the high-altitude balloons. During the second trip, balloon flights 3 and 4 went missing. But of course that wasn't public information. So, when the Roswell story broke, no accurate explanation was ever offered—a fact that only fueled the outlandish rumors. Only decades later, in 1995, did the U.S. military state that the debris found by a rancher and subsequently identified as a "flying disc" by personnel from Roswell Army Air Field was, with a great degree of certainty, the missing Mogul flight number 4, launched on June 4, 1947.

That 1995 military report outlined the true story, paraphrased here, of what really happened near Roswell in 1947:

In mid-June, a rancher named William "Mac" Brazel and his son came across a bright wreckage of rubber strips, tinfoil, tough paper, and sticks that had come to rest on the ranch where he worked near the town of Corona, New Mexico. Early July, Brazel reported his find to the local sheriff, who contacted Roswell Army Air Field, which in turn sent intelligence officers to evaluate the debris. The officers collected a portion of the material and brought it back to Roswell. On July 8, the U.S. Army's Public Information Office released a statement saying that the Army Air Forces had recovered a flying disc.

Brigadier General Roger Ramey ordered airmen to fly the debris to Fort Worth, Texas. Upon viewing the debris, he and his staff recognized remnants of a high-altitude balloon and its metallic radar target. Ramey invited the local press to view and take photographs of the "weather balloon" debris and declared the flying disc report to be a misunderstanding.

Along with the mixed "it's a disc" and "it's a balloon" reports, hieroglyphic-like characters described by seemingly reliable first-hand witnesses further puzzled people and fueled UFO theories. Witnesses recalled that some of the mysterious debris bore small pink and purple motifs that appeared to be some sort of writing that couldn't be deciphered. In truth, it was printed tape that had been manufactured by a toy company during or shortly after World War II, and due to shortages, the resourceful NYU balloon group had used whatever was readily available, including parts for children's playthings.

Yes, there was a cover-up—but not because alien bodies lay among the debris. Mogul was a top secret U.S. Army Air Forces project and the downed high-altitude balloon almost blew its cover. A strict "need-to-know-basis" policy meant that very few people knew of Mogul's objectives. So the reason for the mixed and distorted messages over the years was because no one could talk truthfully and/or knowledgably about the weird stuff that fell out of the sky. In interviews, Spilhaus and Charles Moore, NYU's constant-level balloon project engineer, stated that they were never informed of the classified name "Mogul," nor did they have access to the military's related scientific data. In response to inquiries, project personnel simply said that they were engaged in balloon research.

Cost, security, and practicality eventually led to the disbandment of Mogul. But the project laid a foundation for a comprehensive program in geophysical research. The U.S. military and the scientific community soon capitalized on aspects of the project, including constant-level balloon technology, first developed by Spilhaus's group at NYU.

Before Mogul ended, Athelstan took a six-month leave from balloons and NYU to return to his natal turf to help reorganize the South African meteorological service. The South African government had asked the U.S. State Department for help and expertise, and Francis Reichelderfer, head of the U.S. Weather Service, recommended Spilhaus.

"General Smuts was still Prime Minister," said Spilhaus. "This is the same General Smuts who had interned my father during World War I and then subsequently appointed him ambassador to The Hague. On seeing me, he roared with laughter. He said, 'We ask the mightiest technological nation in the world to send an expert and who do we get, a boy from across the street!' I had only been an American citizen for one year at this time and I was damn proud of my appointment from President Truman."

While helping to make weather predictions more effective and efficient, and introducing his young family to their heritage, Spilhaus obtained a doctoral degree in oceanography from the University of Cape Town in 1948. No doubt his furious work habits warranted a Ph.D., but little fanfare accompanied this pinnacle of academic achievement, especially in comparison to the accolades his work garnered at MIT and Woods Hole.

Once back at NYU, around June 1948, Henry Hartig, head of electrical engineering at the University of Minnesota's Institute of Technology, visited Spilhaus. Hartig wondered if the newly minted doctor would be interested in moving to Minneapolis to become the dean of the institute. Spilhaus recalled, "I, being a typical Easterner, didn't think there was much west of the Hudson River other than the University of Chicago and maybe Caltech. I didn't know about deaning, but I had demonstrated I was a fairly good administrator, so I said, 'Yes, I'd be interested.' Then I promptly forgot all about it."

Spilhaus didn't have a chance to forget for long. Within a month, Lewis Morrill, president of the University of Minnesota, called to ask if he would accept the position if he were offered it. When Dr. Spilhaus received the message that Morrill had run and asked for him, he was at a cocktail party in London where he was serving as a consultant to the U.S. Air Force. Here's how Athel recalled what happened next:

> Six p.m. in London was eleven a.m. in Minneapolis, so I asked the young British Commander if he could put through an urgent call to the University President. . . .
>
> President Morrill, whom I'd get to know and admire later on, accepted the call and asked where I was. I replied that I was in London and he nearly fell off his seat. People didn't just pick up the phone and call from London so casually in those days.
>
> He told me that the Regents were meeting and wanted to know if he could propose me for Dean at the University. "Yes, by all means," I said. "By all means, put me up for it."

3

INTERNATIONALIST IN THE HEARTLAND, 1949–1962

If becoming a dean did not make Spilhaus a typical administrator,
neither did it leave him the same scientist as before.
—**Todd Wildermuth**, *Yesterday's City of Tomorrow:*
The Minnesota Experimental City and Green Urbanism

The ink on Athelstan Spilhaus's doctoral degree barely had time to dry before he leapt from New York to the middle of North America with his family in tow. The impetus for such a counterintuitive move for a latent seafarer was that irresistible invitation to head the University of Minnesota's Institute of Technology, which included the colleges of engineering, mines and metallurgy, architecture, and chemistry. At thirty-seven, he was one of the youngest and least administratively experienced deans at the University of Minnesota but definitely not its most subordinate.

As a dean, Spilhaus offered broad directions and gave his talented department heads considerable leeway to pursue their visions. Dean Spilhaus was unconventional and controversial. Another dean, who opposed Spilhaus's plans for reordering the Institute of Technology, said Spilhaus had "an idea on any topic known to man, including how universities should be organized." Another colleague said, "Spilhaus was a great wanderer. He asked me to become associate dean and I, then, discovered I was really going to have to serve essentially as dean because he was gone so much."

Spilhaus's leadership style was hands-off, and he could hardly sit through department meetings. Maybe his impatience stemmed from his participation on more than sixty boards, committees, and commissions over the course of his tenure there. The rewards for spreading his attention so thin were the ego-stroking envy of his peers and access to logistically difficult destinations like the South Pole, the far side of the Iron Curtain, and the atomic testing grounds in Nevada and New Mexico.

At least theoretically, Dr. Spilhaus lived in Minnesota with his wife and five children, but it is probably more truthful to say that he lived in hotels with a battered attaché and suitcase. The university was lenient with the professor, granting him sixteen leaves of absence during his eighteen-year tenure. He traveled constantly.

"If becoming a dean did not make Spilhaus a typical administrator, neither did it leave him the same scientist as before. When Spilhaus's professional role changed from detector to dean—from scientist to technologist—his publications changed along with it," said historian Todd Wildermuth. "Where before he explored air and water to find new facts, now he probed them for their usefulness to humanity. . . . Discovery had become a precursor to manipulation."

To be fair, other factors might also have precipitated Spilhaus's shift from curious explorer to spokesperson for applied science. More and more, he was debating the impacts of scientific advances on the future of humanity and the environment. In 1951 Spilhaus bore witness to atomic bomb tests in Nevada as a consultant on Operation Buster-Jangle, a Department of Defense and Los Alamos National Laboratory Project evaluating a series of seven nuclear detonations. Spilhaus participated in the Armed Forces Special Weapons Project. Although he declined an invitation to stay on past his nine-month leave of absence from the University,

Atomic testing grounds in Nevada, 1951. Spilhaus served as the scientific director of weapons effects with the Armed Forces Special Weapons Project. Photo courtesy of Corporal McCauhey via Wikimedia Commons.

the U.S. Air Force awarded him an Exceptional Civilian Service medal in 1952 for his role as the scientific director of weapons effects.

Perhaps the audience at the 1953 Mid-Century Conference on Resources for the Future would have noticed Spilhaus's shift in tone toward science. With confidence bordering on arrogance, Spilhaus issued directives for approaching the environment, including climate, with a logical sequence of stages involving observations, understanding, prediction, and ultimately control.

Busy traveling, administering, lecturing, and writing books, Athelstan didn't have much time for inventing new scientific instruments. But his worldliness established his cachet in the heartland, too, enabling some of his novel ideas to find purchase.

For example, today it is possible to stroll through the skyways in downtown Minneapolis because of a Spilhaus idea. After coming up with the concept to foster economic activity by linking buildings in cold-climate cities with enclosed pedestrian walkways and tunnels, Spilhaus then convinced urban planners and politicians to do it.

A Scientist Gets Political

It's necessary to realize that intellectual honesty was not a characteristic of Athelstan Spilhaus: It was his religion!
—**Robert Abel**, founding director of the National Sea Grant Program

Early in his tenure with the University of Minnesota, one of the more pivotal boards the stocky man of science served on was the United Nations Educational, Scientific and Cultural Organization (UNESCO) executive board. Through a presidential appointment by President Dwight Eisenhower in 1954, the dean became the first official U.S. representative to the organization. He claimed he took the job despite his doubts about UNESCO's efficacy because it complemented his University of Minnesota position and because he wanted to offset Russian propaganda associated with the Cold War.

"Representation at UNESCO caused extreme mental conflict to Dr. Spilhaus," Robert Abel would later say. "He had always been a man of immense loyalty, and he was, after all, the first representative of his adopted nation. He was thus honor-bound to advance the United States' position in all matters. One of these positions was to prohibit the entrance of China into the United Nations at all costs. Now Dr. Spilhaus had known, respected, and admired Chairman Mao. . . . Since the Chinese population is the largest in the world, it was ridiculous to keep that country out of the United Nations, to say nothing of UNESCO, which after all represented education, science, and culture."

His involvement in world events consumed his life. Of the many memorable vignettes during his four years with UNESCO, the World Conference in Uruguay was his first. Since the United States and Russia had appropriated the best hotels and the biggest vehicles, Dr. Spilhaus thought it would be prudent to offer rides to representatives from smaller nations. "In those days the Burmese ambassador . . . wore a skirt, while some of the Africans were in leopard skins. Indians wore the Nehru jackets. I'd pick up anybody who was in strange dress," said Spilhaus.

Two of the men he picked up were dressed in "beanies" and "what looked like night dresses." They turned out to be representatives of the Santa Sede, which Athelstan didn't recognize as the Vatican's address. Further evidence of Athelstan's short-lived international naivete was that he thought he heard one of the delegates say his name was Cardinal Martini. Almost giving heart palpitations to the U.S.'s protocol officer, within 48 hours Spilhaus was sipping a dry martini in the company of Cardinal Montini, the future Pope Paul VI. Spilhaus recalled:

> At the U.S. delegation meeting, which we always had at about five o'clock in our hotel, I told the story of "my ride with Martini," just to liven things up a bit. The protocol officer, who had nothing to do, became very upset. He said, "Oh, this is terrible, we may have insulted the Vatican." The protocol officer then explained that Santa Sede was the Holy City. "I'll get a telegram off to [Secretary of State] Dulles, eyes only."
>
> "Nonsense," I said. "We had a good time. I'm sure he's friendly." He mumbled, "Dreadful mistake," and all that. The next morning, hand delivered, came an engraved card inviting me to the papal nunciate, where the Papal Nuncio lives. I showed this to the

protocol officer and said, "Look, in case I goof again, why don't you come along?"

We arrived at the nunciate, walked in the door and joined the receiving line. Both Cardinal Montini—I'd learned his actual name was Montini—and the Papal Nuncio were there. The Cardinal stepped out of the receiving line, came over to me, took both my hands in his and shook them warmly. He said, smiling, "You know, at the residence of the Papal Nuncio, we generally only serve wine, but for you I have a dry martini," and the Swiss Guard brought a silver salver with a lovely frosted cocktail shaker. I said to the protocol officer, "I guess you can go home."

I got to know Cardinal Montini pretty well and we discussed all kinds of things, like birth control and the touchy things with the Catholic Church. After all, we were there for science, education and culture.

In similar fashion, and to the chagrin of U.S. embassy officials, Spilhaus routinely and blithely crossed protocol lines with exuberance, expressing his thoughts with wild abandon. Impatient by nature and weary of UNESCO's inefficiency, Spilhaus evidently announced to the board that their way of doing business was "like elephants making love—done with a great deal of trumpeting at a very high level, and then nothing happens for two years."

During his UNESCO assignments, Spilhaus sought opportunities to tell and retell a favorite story, his lawnmower fable, in speeches and in print. He felt it reflected many of UNESCO's discussions on science and education. The story goes like this:

Originally, the lawnmower was just a cutting reel and two wheels. The grass cuttings went everywhere. A clever fellow developed a bag to collect the cuttings but, after they had been collected, he did not know where to put them. So, he put on his white coat, went into the laboratory with the grass cuttings, and discovered that he could make a drinkable, whitish fluid out of them, and that the residue was useful fertilizer.

The man put a motor on the lawn mower so he didn't have to push it, but the wheels did not negotiate uneven ground. So he installed caterpillar-like walking treads about the same time that he developed onboard equipment to separate the solid fertilizer, which was expelled, and the fluid, which was stored in little pouches.

Finally, he added a modern electronic device, which could sense where the grass was long and could guide the mower. He sat back, satisfied to have reinvented the cow.

Being a UNESCO representative had its honors—and its consequences. Spilhaus was the first American ever asked to serve on that board, which puzzled him until a Czechoslovakian representative told him, "We watched you for two years and determined that you were in fact a true scientist, and not just another State Department stooge." During his service, Dean Spilhaus was elected to UNESCO's executive board with sixty-four out of sixty-five possible votes—and five of these votes came from Soviet bloc representatives.

The UNESCO post, coupled with his wartime experiences in Mao's camp, ultimately landed Spilhaus on a list of possible communists living in the United States. This Red Scare McCarthy-era happenstance was particularly ironic given Spilhaus's raw feelings toward the Kremlin. Later, he recalled that his daughters received a pamphlet at school in St. Paul, "and there was their father being damned as a Communist."

Spilhaus gracefully excused himself from being the U.S. representative to UNESCO in 1958 to commit his time and talent to the National Committee for the International Geophysical Year (IGY): a year-long, worldwide effort to explore the physics of the Earth's geological processes. This, he thought, was much more important than the United Nations' "interminable politicking."

IGY began properly in the summer of 1957, but Spilhaus was involved in its planning from its conception years earlier. (At the 1954 organizational meeting of IGY in Rome, the extroverted Dr. Spilhaus set up his office on a table at a sidewalk café on the Via Veneto, where, he claimed, "everybody passed.") To build excitement and fanfare for IGY research, in 1955 scientists joined presidential press secretary James Hagerty to announce U.S. intentions to build and launch the first-ever man-made satellite into space; these men were Alan Waterman, the first head of the National Science Foundation; Alan Shapley, physicist with the National Bureau of Standards; and Athelstan Spilhaus.

Announcing plans to launch Earth's first artificial satellite, July 29, 1955. Front, left to right: Alan Waterman, James Hagerty, Douglas Cornell, and Alan Shapley. Standing: Wallace Joyce and Athelstan Spilhaus. Photo courtesy of NASA.

Several military branches bickered over the project's ownership until the navy finally won the contract. But the internal strife and posturing slowed the project, which gave Soviet scientists and engineers the chance to preempt America's efforts by putting Sputnik into orbit in October 1957. For many Americans, Sputnik's surprise launch shook their confidence in their own country's scientific prowess. For Spilhaus, the surprise sent him into a dark fury that had him railing against Russia for violating the spirit of IGY and maintaining unwarranted secrecy.

Sputnik vaulted the United States into a frenzy of scientific activity and ambition. By the end of 1957, after the Soviet Union successfully sent a second satellite into orbit—and the U.S. Navy's Vanguard TV3 fizzled on the launch platform—the U.S. government went on a spending spree to push the country's technology, engineering, and science ahead of its Cold War adversaries. The army sent the first U.S. satellite, Explorer 1, into space on January 31, 1958.

While pursuing collaborations for the IGY in Bangkok, Thailand, the ever-opportunistic Spilhaus decided to visit IGY projects in Antarctica. He telegrammed the Antarctica operation and received an invitation to visit McMurdo Sound. The jovial and now savvy diplomat invited a bevy of New Zealanders and Australians, along with a U.S. ambassador, to join the adventure. After whooping it up with martinis stirred with icicles—"The biggest people have the most fun and are not stuffy," Spilhaus claimed—he traveled to Byrd Station and touched the South Pole.

Extending his adventures, Spilhaus next found himself in Russia. Since the point of IGY was to allow scientists from around the world to observe the planet's geophysical phenomena in a détente moment during the Cold War, Dr. Spilhaus joined the American contingent in the territory of an adversarial country he distrusted. Rarely one to kowtow to convention, Spilhaus created a betting game for hotel guests to play as they waited for elevators, and he tipped the maid—an act frowned upon as Western decadence—to ensure an ample supply of hot water, vodka, lemons, and laundry service unobtainable by other hotel guests.

He was well aware that there was still a Cold War going on, but found it impossible to contain his contrarian high spirits. It was obvious to the group that the maid was assigned to keep an eye on them and that their Russian guide tracked their movements— they couldn't go anywhere without her. But he couldn't resist telling the guide that his reason for visiting Lenin's tomb in Red Square, where Stalin's body was also displayed, was to "make damn good and sure they're dead." With that comment, he forfeited his and his navy colleagues' passports, return airline tickets, and extra money for the duration of their visit.

During the International Geophysical Year, Dr. Spilhaus, world traveler extraordinaire, was at home long enough to "give members of the Minneapolis Woman's club a cram course in geophysics and astrophysics," according to a *Minneapolis Star* journalist. Spilhaus had recently returned from Washington, DC, with hope that, after several failed attempts, the United States would be able to reach the moon. Moved to poetry, he quoted his own work:

> Now the moon shows but her face,
> Lovers spoon all over the place.
> What on earth do you think we'd find
> If we looked at her behind?

Despite his eagerness for advances in science, Spilhaus was disturbed by the haste at which some advances were occurring. "By exploding bombs, we have released rare gases into the atmosphere so that we'll never know what the atmosphere was like before the bombs exploded," he said. "By sending a bomb or a dog to the moon, I fear we will contaminate it either with radioactivity or fleas—before we know what it's like."

Spilhaus's concerns were valid. Modern chemists use the mid-twentieth-century "bomb spike" as a milepost in commenting on our planet's recent history.

Our New Age,
1957–1973

Dad's greatest contribution may be the comic strip. —**Fred Spilhaus**

During a UNESCO meeting in Paris, Spilhaus conceived of a project that would amuse him—and a considerable cross-section of humanity—each week for fifteen years. *Our New Age*, the syndicated comic strip he authored, was born of a UNESCO discussion about reading materials for "new literates": adults learning to read. At the meeting, the ambassador from India suggested the United States "stop the exportation of dreadful comic strips," which he felt made up the bulk of the available texts for India's new literates.

Defending the country that had absorbed him, Spilhaus quickly countered that picture-word combinations are the best way for new literates to learn to read. Even the friezes of ancient Egypt and the Bayeux Tapestry in France were, in essence, comic strips, telling the stories of a culture, he said.

When Spilhaus returned to Minnesota, he discussed the UN-ESCO meeting with his friend John Cowles, owner of the *Minneapolis Star* and the *Minneapolis Tribune*. He pitched the idea of writing a science comic strip that encapsulated factual kernels in a husk of entertainment. Cowles agreed and said if Spilhaus wrote it, he would see that it became syndicated.

It took the stunning launch of Sputnik to convince the busy professor-traveler-diplomat to moonlight as a comic strip author. By then, 1957, Spilhaus had left the UNESCO board and was involved with the International Geophysical Year. Especially after Sputnik, Spilhaus considered Russia a duplicitous nation and refused to concede the sky to it. Part of his personal crusade was waged through the Sunday funnies by attempting to ignite scientific fervor in the U.S. populace. Within two years the strip, which could take up a sizable

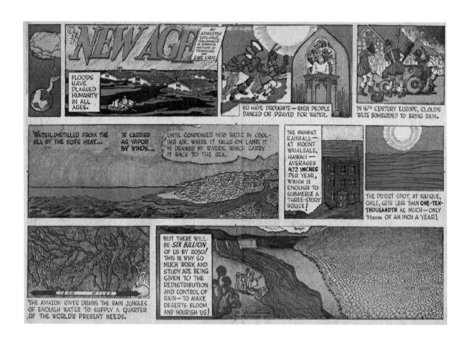

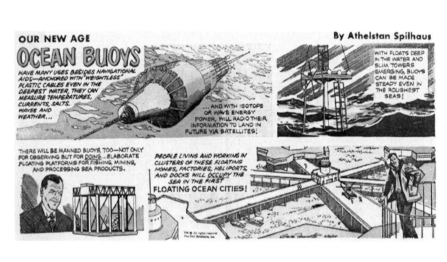

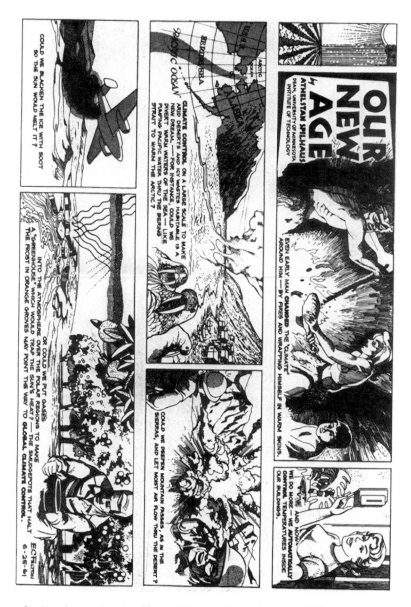

Our New Age comic strips: "Floods," illustrated by Earl Cros, 1959; "Buoys,"
illustrated by Gene Fawcette, 1964; "Climate," illustrated by E. C. Felton, 1961.
Courtesy of Joe Vadus. Reprinted with permission from King Features Syndicate.

chunk of newspaper real estate (14 inches by 9.5 inches), ran in over a hundred newspapers in the United States and nineteen abroad.

Spilhaus wore out three artists in the fifteen years he penned his weekly visions of how science could be applied in the future. Illustrators Earl Cros, E. C. Felton, and Gene Fawcette turned Spilhaus's words into remarkable visions of what might be possible, even if, at times, the "science fact" in the strip teetered on the verge of science fiction. Dr. Spilhaus treated the endeavor as a hobby. Deadlines were demanding and sometime daunting, especially in 1962 when he created a single panel version of the comic on a daily basis. He eventually determined the daily pressure wasn't worth the reward.

The subjects he chose were hopeful and provocative. They dealt with the desalinization of seawater, medicines, cities of the future, computers, agriculture, and much, much more.

"In the years I wrote the strip," Spilhaus recounted, "I ran into one minor secrecy issue." The sensitive topic was the possibility of creating an artificial ionosphere. The strip was based on his own memories of releasing silvery metallic chaff during World War II bombing runs to confuse enemy radars. Spilhaus didn't know about Project West Ford (aka Project Needles). Through that classified project, MIT scientists were working with the U.S. military in the early 1960s to create an artificial ionosphere to stabilize the communications signals bouncing off the Earth's natural ionosphere. When military intelligence officers came knocking, Spilhaus was nonplused by their suspicion that he had heard about the project at a secret meeting and now was telling the world about it.

At its zenith, the *Our New Age* strip ran in 137 Sunday newspapers worldwide, including Spilhaus's natal land of South Africa. During a visit to South Africa, a tavern-owning newspaper columnist asked Dr. Spilhaus when he found the time to write the strips. He answered, "Why, when I'm not writing opinions on geophysical problems for the American government, or TV talks or lectures, or flying off to board meetings which occupy much of my time. An idea comes to me as I travel or as I talk to you and I jot it down." Was he running out of ideas? "Not at all," he told the columnist. "Ideas crowd in. Scientific advances are being made faster than I can use them."

And, as always, Spilhaus made an impression with his physicality as well as his intellect. The tavern owner described Athelstan as resembling a ship's captain, an "open-air man, short, powerful, sun-tanned." Another observer called him "a chubby cheerful man of science."

He wasn't running out of ideas for his own amusement, either. In 1959 Dr. Spilhaus told a *Time* magazine reporter, "I love to try something I don't know how to do and then damn well do it." That year he was also taking up trap drumming, dabbling in abstract painting, and learning about business. A fellow professor said, "Spilhaus is swinging in wider and wider orbit, so that people have a chance to get over being mad before he gets back to them."

Spilhaus opted to cease writing the strip in 1973. By that time he was settling down in Middleburg, Virginia, and was involved with another creative project: conceptualizing and fabricating the *Sun Triangle*, a public sculpture that still stands in New York City.

Childlike in some ways himself, Athel could be difficult as a father. Fred remembered his father insisting on being the center of attention and insisting on driving while intoxicated (he was issued at least one DUI, on May 20, 1950). "I guess when I was a kid, what used to annoy me more than anything else was that he not only had a disdain for rules, but he liked to flout them," Fred said. "If a restaurant said coat and tie required, he would deliberately take his coat and tie off and leave it in the car. Or, they'd throw him out, and he'd go out to the car and he'd take his shirt off, put his tie and his coat on, and insist that we all go back in the restaurant. There was a point in my life when I actually would stay in the car. I wouldn't eat with them in restaurants. He would do something that would be tremendously embarrassing. My mother went along.

I mean, she was married to him and she must have known what she was getting into, to some extent at least."

Meet Me at the Fair (or the Beach)

Science is one of the highest forms of entertainment. —**Athelstan Spilhaus**

In addition to dashing about the globe, Spilhaus began designing clocks during the late 1950s. His actions weren't random or whimsical, however. He aimed at solving a problem: when his family was vacationing by the sea, they needed a timepiece that indicated the

Spilhaus Space Clock. Photo courtesy of Kathy Spilhaus.

ocean tides so Mary could plan family meals and other activities accordingly. It took him about six years to invent and perfect the Spilhaus Space Clock, which President Lyndon Johnson gave out as presentation gifts to certain visiting dignitaries.

Housed in a wooden cabinet, it sported three faces. Two small faces showed the time: one on a standard twelve-hour dial, one on a twenty-four hour dial indicating the time in major cities around the world. The large face—the "space dial"—showed five overlaid discs, each mapped with astronomical data. Together, they displayed fourteen bits of celestial information, such as:

- position of the sun, moon, and stars
- month and day
- sidereal (star) time
- moon phase
- time of sunrise and sunset, moonrise and moonset, and star rise and star set
- time of high and low tides and the stage of the tide

Edmund Scientifics manufactured the space clock from 1964 to 1976, selling it for $150—expensive for its day. The accompanying booklet, titled *Lots of Time*, noted that it was "considered by many to be a breakthrough in the art and science of clock making."

Indeed, Spilhaus seemed to work on the frontier of several fields at any given time. While he was based in Minnesota, many people asked Dr. Spilhaus how he could be drawn into so many careers at the same time: serving as dean of the Institute of Technology, writing a syndicated comic strip, and making clocks; not to mention his international contributions and efforts on national defense. But Spilhaus didn't feel like the endeavors were different at all.

"I don't do 'so many things.' I do one. I think about the future," he said to his friend Victor Cohn, the *Minneapolis Tribune* and

Minneapolis Star beat reporter who went on to become one of the nation's most famous medical journalists.

The future was certainly on his mind when he took a yearlong leave of absence from the University of Minnesota to salvage the U.S. science exhibit at the Seattle World's Fair at the behest of President Kennedy.

Jerome Wiesner, President Kennedy's scientific advisor and later president of MIT, called Spilhaus with the request in the spring of 1961. He persuaded the worldly Spilhaus to take the appointment—U.S. Commissioner to the Seattle World's Fair—in part by arranging for him to talk personally to President Kennedy.

Spilhaus recounted, "I was in Guana Cay in the Bahamas, an out island, very primitive, where the telephone communication was an on-and-off thing, only twice a day, a half hour in the morning and a half hour in the afternoon. A call came through to the operator asking for Dr. Spilhaus. The operator said, 'The doc don't get up this early.'" The caller was Jerome Wiesner. The operator told Wiesner that the president would have to call between 3:00 and 3:30 p.m. The whole island was excited.

Spilhaus, who owned part of the Cay, said, "At 3:30, all the school children were sitting around the radio as my call came in asking me to come to Washington to talk to the president about running the Seattle World's Fair. I told him I would be there in two days when I finished my fishing. He made some comment about people usually responding *immediately* to a call from the president."

Spilhaus's talents for vision, creativity, scientific inquiry, action, and communication shone brightly in this venue. Although he enjoyed the limelight and the presidential appointment, the Seattle World's Fair challenged Spilhaus. He had only about a year to pull it off: the fair's opening date was April 21, 1962. Knowing that he had a bit of leverage, he threatened to quit when red tape became too thick or cash too scarce. By the time the fair opened its doors, Spilhaus had handed in his resignation three times.

In retrospect, he claimed the experience was "great fun," probably because his position on the board of the American Association for the Advancement of Science ensured that first-rate scientists devoted time to making sure the exhibits were accurate. Spilhaus favored scientists who understood that a dash of showmanship would engage a wider public audience. "I decided the approach to our exhibit should be entertaining as well as educational," he said. "Science is one of the highest forms of entertainment. We hoped to entertain adults and children with the exhibit, and if they were educated by it, fine. Education was not the intent of the exhibit—entertainment was."

When Seattle's civic leaders had begun planning the World's Fair in the mid-1950s, they imagined a "Festival of the West." But, as time passed, the Fair became a vehicle for showing that the United States' science and space technologies were competitive with the Soviet Union's. With the space race underway, and Seattle being an "aerospace city" thanks to Boeing, the change of theme

Spilhaus wanted visitors to the Science Pavilion to be excited by science and technology, 1962. Photo courtesy of the Seattle Municipal Archives.

was almost inevitable. The technology-based optimism on display assumed that American affluence, automation, consumerism, and power would grow. It assumed, as did Spilhaus, that humans would master nature through technology.

The fair—also known as the Century 21 Exposition—and its Science Exhibit were breathtakingly phenomenal. In the World of Science portion of the fair that Athelstan oversaw, artists and scientists labored side by side in a creative frenzy. Boeing donated the spacearium, an eight-ton aluminum dome inside the Science Pavilion, where up to 750 visitors could be awed by a twelve-minute simulated dash through the solar system and beyond. General Electric demonstrated how to make synthetic diamonds. The bomb shelter in the Yamasaki building became a children's room.

Fair organizers were aghast when, for the multiple-series introductory film in the U.S. science pavilion, even the VIP guests were expected to sit cross-legged on the carpet: the shah of Iran, Julian Huxley, and Prince Philip of England. Spilhaus vehemently insisted that foreign dignitaries and special guests experience the pavilion and exhibits in the same fashion as everybody else. Although he imagined people would stand for the film, he appreciated that people were doing something he didn't anticipate. Athelstan's attitude during this time echoed the playful spirit he attempted to inject into the fair.

Once the fair had started, Spilhaus assumed the role of greeter for distinguished visitors. Typically a martini man, he decided to imbibe only wine and beer, given how much entertaining he was doing.

With an eye for publicity, Spilhaus announced that the children's science room was for children only, and adults were allowed only if accompanied by children. This produced a story, possibly a true one, that entrepreneurial youngsters were hiring themselves out as escorts. When the story made it into newspapers, Spilhaus enlarged the article to poster size and hung it outside the entrance to generate even more interest in the room's contents.

Spilhaus (left) and Julian Huxley, Seattle World's Fair, 1962. Photo by Ted Bronsten, courtesy of Kathy Spilhaus.

During the fair year, Spilhaus waged a campaign against the Government Services Administration, which typically removed World's Fair buildings after the event. "I just fought, bled, and died to leave everything for Seattle," said Spilhaus. Backed by the clout of two senators, Spilhaus evidently breathed a sigh of relief as the Science Pavilion was transferred into the hands of Seattle and Washington State to endure as the permanent Pacific Science Center. Two Seattle locals were able to save the auditorium, monorail, Space Needle, and other facilities. As a result, the area remains an important convention and cultural center.

Spilhaus, punning that he was an "artificial Seattleite," had been living on a houseboat in the city for over a year by the end of the fair, giving heart and soul to the project. After the fair ended, he asked President Kennedy, "Why did you pick on me?"

Kennedy, who was unable to attend the fair because of the Cuban missile crisis, responded, "The only science I know, Spilly, is what I read in the *Boston Globe* in your comic strip."

The success of his comic strips and the science exhibits at the fair made Spilhaus aware of how little scientific information was otherwise available to the general public. His tack was to lure people to science through the things they loved. In the case of the *Our New Age*, it was the comics. In the case of the World's Fair, it was Japanese gardens, fountains, and thrilling music.

By the end of the fair, Spilhaus, at age fifty, was wildly successful professionally, but his marriage was foundering. He had been traveling extensively, living on a Seattle houseboat, dashing to Washington, DC, and leaving Mary to raise their children in Minnesota. When he was home, it was a culture shock; he often dined separately from the family, dizzied by the chaos that a brood of five could create. Retrospectively admitting to hubris and a post-fair midlife crisis, he encouraged Mary to file for a divorce after he returned to the university. She did. He got Michigan Island in Lake Superior and the house in the Bahamas. She retained the house in St. Paul, 70 acres, a beach home in Massachusetts, and a cottage on Martha's Vineyard. Despite the heartache, evidently Mary loved Athel until death, maintaining that he made life exciting.

Ever impatient, days after his divorce from Mary became final in early 1964, Athel wed Gail Thompson Griffin, a chic businesswoman he had befriended in Seattle eighteen months earlier.

Inspired by all that he had seen and discussed with futurists and architects during the World's Fair, Dr. Spilhaus now began envisioning experimental cities that would not create waste.

"As early as 1961, Athelstan Spilhaus was telling anyone who would listen how irritated he was by pollution, and not just by pollution itself . . . but by the very *idea* of pollution," wrote Wildermuth. "'Waste,' he exhorted, 'is some useful substance which we don't know how to use or which we don't yet know how to use economically.'"

Athelstan's intellectual pursuits, and his rage against waste, brought him to the office of Frederick Seitz, president of the National Academy of Sciences, with ideas about transforming societal waste into reusable resources. Seitz discussed the idea with President Kennedy, who in turn funded a new committee that Dr. Spilhaus presided over: the Committee on Pollution of the National Academy of Sciences and National Research Council. (If Spilhaus had his "cheeky way," the committee might have been called the National Committee on Junk Science.)

Coming from an engineer's perspective, Dr. Spilhaus felt that the committee should focus on causes and innovation, not doom as a foregone conclusion. Thus he insisted that the pollution committee's 1966 report be more pragmatically titled *Waste Management and Control*. He chose twelve people to serve as the core of this committee, people he loosely referred to as "Nobel Prize winners and garbage collectors," six of each. The "garbage collectors" were people like the president of a Los Angeles company that collected thousands of dead animals off the streets each night, rendering their tissues for products such as birdseed cakes. Mixing disparate groups of people, whether artists and scientists or garbage men and Nobel laureates, always intrigued Spilhaus. He considered such collaborations better than those including only practical or theoretical minds.

The waste report garnered congressional attention, and it clearly bore Athel's stamp. The years spent discussing waste, reading about it, and writing about it drove Dr. Spilhaus to conclude that reconfiguring waste management in an old, established city was simply not possible. Maybe the conclusion also stemmed from the professor's new focus. The grandest vision of Spilhaus's life, the Minnesota Experimental City, was rooted in the same soil that led to that 1966 *Waste Management and Control* report. Produced by the national committee he chaired, it prominently recommended that a "full-scale experimental residue-control system be planned, designed, and constructed in a new city." That city—a huge, experimental new prototype for human settlement—was a Spilhaus obsession for at least five years. Known as MXC for short, it was planned in detail and came very close to being built in Aitkin County, Minnesota.

4

MXC, 1962–1973

Until the end Spilhaus insisted that the City was a pure experiment, that it could take whatever shape was necessary to discover new truths and test new technologies. —**Todd Wildermuth**, *Yesterday's City of Tomorrow: The Minnesota Experimental City and Green Urbanism*

The idea for the Minnesota Experimental City (MXC) gelled out of a slurry of visions for reinventing waste management, water use, public transit, and all the systems that make a city function. Dr. Spilhaus abhorred the idea of waste, seeing it as just something we haven't been creative enough to use. He also valued energy as the "fundamental currency of civilization." The modular experimental city he imagined would honor his core principles about waste and energy while helping to stem the troubling tide of people vacating city centers for a glamorized 1960s lifestyle in suburbia. (Ironically, Spilhaus spoke and wrote about the cultural and ecological perils of suburbia, or the "slurbs," while purchasing a home there in 1964.)

According to Spilhaus's vision, MXC was to be one mighty research laboratory, a technocracy where scientific inquiries and prototypes were sovereign. With complete material and water recycling and no internal combustion engines, its 250,000 people would inhabit an extraordinary and revolutionary city that would be a prototype for others of its ilk. The technologies developed and tested in northern Minnesota would attract an international market that would bolster the nation's economy and scientific prowess.

Over the course of his life, people with muscle and money took Dr. Spilhaus seriously and endeavored to chisel his ideas into tangible forms, even extravagant ideas like MXC. Spilhaus had patents, publications, and a personality that enabled him to leverage power. Within a decade, the Experimental City was a shovel or two away from becoming a reality. The story of what happened and what didn't happen is a story about human nature—both Athelstan's and people's in general.

"The younger Spilhaus, the Spilhaus before Minnesota and before the war, had been a master detective, an eager student of environmental discovery," said Todd Wildermuth. "His earliest studies were exercises in exposing natural phenomena, his early inventions aimed to extend the human ability to detect such phenomena. As dean, however, he changed his relationship to basic science. He shifted roles from finder of fact to user of it. Concurrently and perhaps necessarily, his approach to his former research medium, the outdoors itself, changed. Where before he explored air and water to find new facts, now he probed them for their usefulness to humanity. . . . Discovery had become a precursor to manipulation."

Soon after he returned to Minnesota from the World's Fair in Seattle, Dr. Spilhaus began talking about experimental cities, *experimental* being the operative word. His proposed city (and later, cities) would be as close to technology's cutting edge as possible. This vision would occupy him from 1962 until he left Minnesota in 1967. "During those critical years, he created the idea and gave it a name, worked out its broad design, and retained nearly complete control," wrote Wildermuth.

Spilhaus's experiences in Seattle, as well as his consultations on the 1967 Montreal World's Fair, begat friendships with innovators like Moshe Safdie, an Israeli architect who pondered nature's designs in his own way. The push for thinking about cities in a brand new way in the early 1960s was not unique to Spilhaus, but the way he thought about them was uniquely his own: as an experiment, not as a capitalistic endeavor.

Despite expecting that MXC would be a flexible experiment, Athelstan insisted that certain characteristics were immutable: MXC had to be placed far from existing metropolitan areas; "it had to be populated by hundreds of thousands and not a mere village; it had to allow for constant rearrangement without any emotional attachments to the past."

The Experimental City, according to Spilhaus, needed to be at least 100 miles from any major urban center, with vast tracts of unoccupied surrounding land. He felt it was important to keep

The proposed location of MXC, circa 1965. Sketch courtesy of University of Minnesota, Andersen Library, Archives and Special Collections.

MXC from becoming another city's bedroom community. Plumbing, communication, police protection, firefighters, and medical professionals would be strategically placed in this new city, rather than an inserted afterthought. Spilhaus reasoned that when a boat is built, everything to take care of the passengers is installed before the people come aboard and that a city could, and maybe should, be built in a similar way.

Even long after the MXC concept was abandoned, Spilhaus held on to his vision. He said, "I dream of a city which is essentially a non-building city, where the shelters are adequate and flexible, but the services to people are maximum and glorious. The city of the future will no longer be for the exchange of things. It will be primarily for the exchange of ideas. We still need to build an experimental city. No one would want to fly in an airplane of which a prototype had not been built. Would anyone live in a city of which a prototype, an experimental model, had not been built?"

Looking back on 1962, however, Spilhaus admitted to letting his logical engineering imagination run free. "It was natural for me to think about how to improve the function of city services through fundamental city planning," he said. " . . . Part of the concept was also not to allow the city to grow. . . . A major problem of cities is cancerous unplanned growth. Very few cities are fully planned; only the hearts are planned. L'Enfant planned the streets of Washington, DC, so a cannon could command all the roads coming in. Today a single disabled automobile can affect all the roads that come into Washington."

Dr. Spilhaus observed that unplanned development typically precedes sewers, roads, telephone lines, schools, law enforcement systems, and the like. "Therefore, all the essential human services—the way we do it in the United States and most other places in the world—must lag behind the given needs," he said. "Cities have to wait for human needs to become acute before they can even make a pitch for these things."

Spilhaus envisioned an underground level for the services that cause distress or annoyance in cities—"the screaming ambulances, the police cars, the fume-belching automobiles, the necessary services" with "fume sewers" and vents to expel the gasses. There too he would install modular piping and conduits for the wastes, as well as gas and electrical services. Ground level would be for foot traffic and buildings. Echoing the monorail in Seattle, mass transit systems would be one level above the ground.

Many aspects of typical urban design didn't make sense to Dr. Spilhaus. One vexation was the way water is used for waste. The oceanographer in him couldn't resist pointing out that the amount of water on the planet stays constant, cycling on a mammoth scale; he thought it was time for man to echo nature's water cycle on a city scale. It struck him as ridiculous that we take water from natural systems, mix it with "good human organic fertilizer," and then build costly treatment plants to separate the components back into river water and sludge for fertilizer. It seemed to him that urban planners kept finding new and ever more expensive ways to waste water and other resources. He thought the Experimental City could eliminate such nonsense. His idea for the commode was to suck out the waste out of the system with pneumatics using a minimum of water. This idea was eventually tested in experimental units in Europe and toilets with pneumatic flushing are now common in Sweden and in eco-minded homes around the world.

The rationale behind aiming for 250,000 occupants in MXC reflected Spilhaus's logical approach to accommodating the country's growing population. Dr. Spilhaus calculated that the nation added about three million people each year—twelve times his imaginary city's population size. He observed that "these people are taken care of with no planning at all." He thought that building a planned city for them would cost about $2 billion (in 1966 dollars). To build *his* planned city, he suggested doubling the figure to $4 billion to account for the experimental nature of the design.

At this time, the well-connected Spilhaus had a role with the U.S. Department of Housing and Urban Development (HUD). "I was on a HUD advisory committee, chaired by my good friend George McGee, and presented my Experimental City idea to them," Spilhaus recalled. "Skeptics asked, 'Where do you get the front money?' I said, 'You give your little loans, figure it $20,000 apiece for 250,000 people, and you get something like $5 billion. That's what I need. Why can't HUD, instead of keeping all its people busy writing little loans of $20,000, write me a loan for [$5 billion]?'"

A $5 billion investment in MXC didn't fly with HUD, although philosopher of technology Lewis Mumford and futurist R. Buckminster Fuller thought the idea had a chance. Spilhaus's concept also garnered the support of other heavy hitters, including economist Walter Heller, urbanologist Harvey Perloff, and Constantinos Doxiadis, a famous Greek city planner. But the biggest boon for the Experimental City concept came in the form of Otto Silha,

A model of MXC, circa 1965. Photo courtesy of University of Minnesota, Andersen Library, Archives and Special Collections.

president and publisher of the Minneapolis Star and Tribune Company.

Spilhaus was regularly interviewed and quoted by Silha's reporters, and his comic strip ran in Silha's papers. Wildermuth speculates that the two men likely knew each other even before the 1965 memo Silha sent to Spilhaus summarizing a meeting with Vice President Hubert Humphrey. Nevertheless, their documented association began with that memo and MXC. Within fourteen months, the dynamic duo and their partners were ready to launch a nationally syndicated five-part newspaper series promoting the project, authored by Spilhaus, and a preliminary Experimental City proposal to federal agencies. Within another nine months they had secured $248,000 in federal funding. Humphrey, a fan of the project, marveled that the MXC team was populated by retired four-star General Bernard Schriever; Athelstan Spilhaus, "one of the greatest minds that God ever put on two shoulders"; and the tenacious Otto Silha.

As Wildermuth pointed out in his dissertation, the MXC *idea* was Spilhaus's, but the MCX *project* was "undeniably Silha's." Silha was originally interested in developing a new city from an entrepreneurial standpoint, rather like Hershey, Pennsylvania, or even a fully enclosed city like Disney's Epcot. Epcot, a name many know and love, is an acronym for "Experimental Prototype Community of Tomorrow." Between 1962 and 1964, Walt Disney himself was planning this utopia next to his Florida theme park. As if channeling MXC, Disney said he envisioned a never-complete prototype community built with advanced designs and new technologies. Even though the utopian dream evaporated after Walt Disney's death, a version of Epcot has remained popular since it opened in 1982.

Faced with competition from tycoons like Disney, Silha opted to merge his dream city with Spilhaus's experimental one in order to make successful pitches for government backing and seed money. It worked. The group's enthusiasm and salesmanship ignited people in Washington, DC, and the Minnesota state legislature, which in turn softened the labor unions' resolve to uphold existing building and engineering codes. As a top executive with the biggest newspaper company in Minnesota, Otto Silha knew how to hold an audience once their attention was drawn.

According to Spilhaus, Buckminster Fuller wanted to enclose "the whole damn thing in one of his geodesic domes." Fuller became famous for working out the engineering principles that allowed the popularization of geodesic domes, surprisingly strong sphere-like structures composed of a network of triangles made out of a minimum of materials. Later, Athel said, "I had to keep Buck happy because he was worthwhile for his ideas and I had to keep him on my team."

Spilhaus's relationship with Fuller wasn't completely adversarial, nor was it as warm as Spilhaus sometimes made it out to be. They disagreed on the use of geodesic domes and the value of unfettered wind. Athelstan felt he was practical while Fuller was visionary. "Bucky was a genius," Spilhaus said. "He did not steal ideas from me. He stole from Plato. The geodesic dome was his patent, which was one of Plato's solids, the polyhedron, which Plato played with two thousand years ago. It's only a genius that can patent a thing that is two thousand years old."

It could be that Spilhaus didn't care to compete for attention. If anyone was more eccentric and charismatic than Athel himself, it might have been Bucky. "He ate an absolutely regular diet of coffee, steak, potatoes and ate that meal three times a day," Athel recalled. "He charmed the young with his imaginative ideas. When asked to talk for one hour, he talked for three hours. He had a brand of math he called synergistic and energistic geometry, which neither I nor any mathematician could understand."

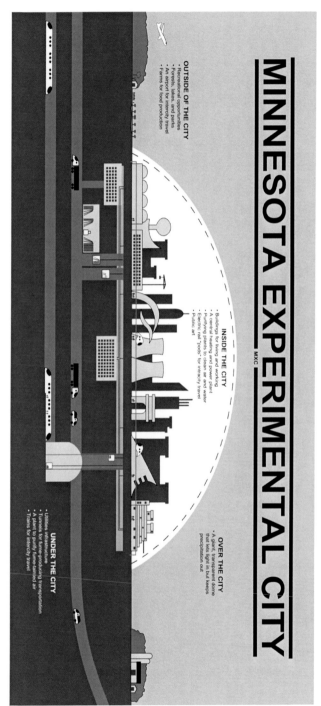

MINNESOTA EXPERIMENTAL CITY

MXC

OUTSIDE OF THE CITY
- Recreational opportunities
- Forests, lakes, and parks
- An airport for intercity travel
- Farms for food production

INSIDE THE CITY
- Buildings for living and working
- A central heating and power plant
- Purifying plants to clean air and water
- Electric rail "pods" for intercity travel
- Public art

OVER THE CITY
- A giant, transparent dome that lets light in but keeps precipitation out

UNDER THE CITY
- Utilities infrastructure
- Tunnels for fume-producing transportation
- A plant to purify fume-tainted air
- Trains for intercity travel

Vision of what the Experimental City might look like. Illustration by Russell Habermann, Minnesota Sea Grant.

Spilhaus, creator of the MXC idea, and Silha, a practical appli-
cator of ideas, spearheaded the early years of developing the plan
of what the Experimental City might become. Especially in 1967,
Spilhaus stumped tirelessly for MXC. His rhetoric included his
expectations for the new city to serve as an international proving
ground for urban technologies that could be exported.

In an article published in *Newsweek* in 1968, Athelstan reportedly
said at a meeting of the American Association for the Advancement of Science, "Without exception our cities are hopelessly
bound by tradition, outmoded building codes, restrictive legislation and the abortions of their historical development." He spoke
of inflatable buildings, saying. "An obsolete building should dis-
appear like uneaten ice cream in a cone . . . draining out through
the . . . bottom."

In his mind, the modular über-modern city would thrive on a
constant flow of research and technological development. For this
to happen, he said, three goals must be acknowledged: the need
to control the size of urban populations, the need for individuals
to become psychologically (and therefore also financially) detached
from their things and their history, and unapologetic technocracy.
The more he talked, the clearer it became that his ideas were somewhat different than Silha's and, frankly, somewhat removed from
the reality of living in a city inhabited by actual people. Because
his MXC colleagues could not applaud all of his ideas, Athelstan
became irritated with them as the meetings and the years went by.
Especially toward the end, he often left meetings in a foul mood.

The Experimental City's broad appeal rested on its goals of
solving two crises: the decay of the nation's inner cities and the
potential for environmental disaster through unplanned growth
and pollution. It also resonated with the anxieties and dreams of
the times. According to Wildermuth, "the City was a seed that had
a chance only because it was planted in the fertile, upturned soil of
the 1960s." Had there been no rioting in inner cities and no rivers

catching fire, the MXC concept would probably not have come as close as it did to becoming real.

The momentum for the Experimental City slowed and then stopped for a number of reasons. Spilhaus understood that he was a philosopher of city planning, rather than a doer. "I have great sympathy for the doers, because I'm not very good at translating ideas into practice," he wrote. "I've taken on the challenge on occasion, but I don't enjoy it. Unfortunately, after I moved to Philadelphia, the project bogged down. The legislature, instead of voting the money, voted to have tertiary treatment plants for sewage."

Spilhaus, after conceptualizing and tirelessly advocating for the Experimental City, rapidly lost his energy for it when he became the president of Philadelphia's Franklin Institute in 1967. He came back to MCX planning meetings in Minnesota on several occasions, but in May 1968 he resigned as co-chair of the MCX project and in June 1969 he met with the group for the last time.

Around the time Athelstan was excusing himself from any further MCX planning, the Minnesota House and Senate authorized a needs and assessment study of the Minnesota Experimental City. Soon after, a national committee formed and began acting as a steering committee to guide five phases of development. Moving into phase two by 1971, the Minnesota legislature authorized an eleven-member MXC Authority. As time went on, more money was raised: Northern States Power, Pillsbury, Honeywell, and the Minneapolis Star and Tribune Company joined with state foundations and the American Gas Association to generate about $670,000 for designing MXC, while Ford Motor Company spent $300,000 on a transportation study.

So where is this fabulous city? Where is this domed venue for experiments with human psychology, society, and technology? Experts attribute some of MXC's failure to launch to Spilhaus. Reflecting his core values, Spilhaus viewed science and technology as innately good; he welcomed radical change; and he was comfortable with engineers and scientists making decisions about public welfare. Evidently, the more design details he included in the MXC concept, the fewer departures he could tolerate.

But Spilhaus's reported cantankerous and rigid attitude alone didn't sink the plans. Locating the project brought additional complications. With appropriate money, backers, labor unions, and legislation at the ready, the Experimental City site of about 75,000 acres was chosen near Swatara, a lightly populated area in Aitkin County in north central Minnesota. Many residents embraced the opportunity, which would offer employment in a sparse financial landscape. In 1972 the Aitkin County Board voted unanimously in favor of courting the MXC project, but the general enthusiasm was short-lived. Rapid and vehement opposition developed from the Minnesota Pollution Control Agency (MPCA), environmental groups, and community activists.

The Minnesota Legislature had formed the MPCA in 1967 to protect the state's air, water, and land; in February 1973 the agency "sought to protect its newly acquired bureaucratic turf." What the MPCA billed as an orderly public meeting in St. Paul became a public hearing and inquisition on the Experimental City, to which MXC spokesman and project manager Jim Alcott objected, "We obviously did not come prepared for this particular type of questioning." To this, in essence, the MPCA officials and people in the room responded, "Too bad," and proceeded to find the MXC Authority guilty of subterfuge and elitism, of not involving Aitkin County residents, of keeping the details of the city secret, and of intending to destroy marshlands. True, the MXC Authority didn't involve the people most likely to be affected by the Experimental City until near the end of the game, and when they did, they fumbled.

A 1973 article in *Time* magazine suggested the new city could create 130,000 new jobs and capture the imagination of city planners around the world; meanwhile, rivals of the *Minneapolis Star* and

Tribune empire were printing editorials in vehement opposition to the Experimental City. The slanderous editorials in early February punctuated the beginning of a span that Spilhaus referred to as "get Spilhaus and his ideas month."

Years later, when interviewing Dr. Spilhaus, Louise O'Connor reported that talking about the 1973 editorials and the end of MXC threw him into "a tirade far too voluminous to print." She paraphrased his rant this way: "Everyone seemed to miss the point of experimentation and trial and looked at the idea from the usual [rote] method of thinking. Everyone in these news stories fusses about the ideas and has no optimism for working it out, just a blind 'No, can't do' attitude."

After years of enthusiastic support from scientists, the media, and legislators, and hundreds of hours of planning, the eleven-year-old project died in 1973. However, some of the ideas generated through conceptualizing the Experimental City—such as pneumatic sewage systems and pollution management technologies—have been applied in France, Sweden, and Japan. Others may yet find that their time has come.

Later in his life, Spilhaus explored the experimental city idea in a different way by advocating for settlements beneath the ocean's surface. (Incidentally, Buckminster Fuller designed a floating city that never came to fruition and that didn't involve Dr. Spilhaus.) Spilhaus was aware that a sea-based city could operate beyond what he viewed as the suffocating laws governing the use of land.

"The question of cities in the sea is a concept much less defensible than experimental cities on land and far more difficult to create," he said. "Yet, with the extreme laws we have on pollution and environmental impact, a city in the sea, where people could use all the cooling water they needed from the sea and could use their organic waste for fertilizing aquaculture, would be very efficient."

Athelstan was visionary but also a pragmatic collector of ideas. Because of his global networking, he likely knew about Le Corbusier's 1920s unrealized city for three million (Ville Contemporaine) and Frank Lloyd Wright's pipe dream (Broadacre City, circa 1932). He was probably no stranger to the Metabolist movement started in 1959 by Japanese architects and city planners who visualized cities of flexible and extensible structures like the floating city idea of Unabara. Maybe he felt the rumblings of mid-century city designs like Epcot in Florida and "new towns" or "techno-cities" like Le Vaudreuil in France and Neue Heimat in Germany. He clearly embraced the future. He once told an interviewer, "I'm impatient with the past and irritable with the present. The future is where my concern lies, and I'm very optimistic about it."

5
SEA GRANT,
1963–TODAY

The concept of Sea Grant Colleges which you described
nearly a decade ago has resulted in the development over the
past five years of one of the most productive and innovative
programs in recent Federal history. —**Richard Nixon**,
in a letter from the White House, October 5, 1972

While going through a divorce and acquiring a new bride,
writing a regular comic strip, and catapulting the Experimental City idea into the hearts and minds of politicians, engineers, and urban planners, Dr. Spilhaus also somewhat carelessly
lobbed another idea that would commandeer equally vast quantities of his time and energy: Sea Grant.

"Oceans are not a dry subject," Spilhaus had once quipped to
Jacques Cousteau, one of his few equals in passion for the sea. He
really meant it, though, and he thought, wrote, and spoke about
oceans so frequently that Lloyd Smith, a professor at the University
of Minnesota and chair of the 1963 American Fisheries Society
conference, invited him to give a keynote address at the annual
meeting in Minneapolis. (Later, Dr. Smith served as Minnesota
Sea Grant's original director for the year before his death.)

At the time, Spilhaus was a bit restless, finding the "deaning
bureaucracy boring" after living the World's Fair life in Seattle.

"That sort of power and position had gone to my head," he said later, recalling his invitation to give the keynote speech, "and I fell for a very short time into the error of thinking: 'Oh, hell, I'm such a good speaker, I don't have to prepare this thing, I'll just do it off-the-cuff.' That is the worst mistake even the brightest man in the world can make. Anyone can prepare very carefully and then throw away the script. That's OK. But for heaven's sake, never go up there unprepared.

"There I was, quite literally, going from my home in St. Paul in a taxi, because I wanted to think and get prepared ahead of time, to the hotel where this meeting was being held in Minneapolis. I was thinking, what will I tell these people on a boring subject, an age-old one? How do we get government, industry, and the universities to cooperate? And I suddenly thought, here's the University of Minnesota, a land grant institution, and . . . and . . . *land grant*! . . . Those wise men over a hundred years ago invented a way of drawing the research from the botany departments, from the little physics departments, and increasing the hybridization of corn, or doing whatever was necessary to improve agriculture, using the mechanic arts to perfect our early agricultural machinery, and making the United States preeminent in the growing and harvesting of food for people. Once that went through my mind, I thought, what the hell, that's the way to do it for the *sea*."

On that September morning a few minutes later, he was extemporizing to the fisheries managers and researchers gathered at the Pick-Nicollet Hotel. He began by tapping into their concerns about commercial fishing. "We worry about the Russians taking fish off the Grand Banks. I think our worry, if we admit it in our heart of hearts, is that they are doing an efficient job and we are not," he said. And they resonated with his outrage when he reminded them how Peruvian ships outfished all other nations, and how the United States was outfished by Japan on the East Coast and the Soviet Union on the West Coast. Although U.S. fishermen sought regulations to protect the nation's fisheries, now Spilhaus suggested an alternative: cultivate more competitive fisheries by investing in research that involved academia, state agencies, federal agencies, and industry.

His listeners were riveted. Spilhaus knew the audience loved the notion that, like land grant's grassroots program, they could create an "eelgrass roots" effort for the sea. "I made up my presentation as I went along," he said later. "It was very imaginative and just gripped the audience."

Spilhaus's off-the-cuff September speech would develop into a national program that still serves America's coastal communities.

An Idea Comes of Age—Quickly

Just as we have county agents going out from university to the farm, we'll have county agents in hip boots going out to drilling rigs, going out with trawlers. —**Athelstan Spilhaus**

As a dean at a land-grant university like the University of Minnesota, Spilhaus was aware that, a century earlier, the United States Congress had stimulated the practical study of agriculture, science, engineering, mechanic arts and military tactics when it passed the Morrill Act establishing a land-grant fund. Though President Buchanan vetoed the Act in 1857, Lincoln signed it in 1862, setting the stage for the country's preeminence in military pursuits and the mass production of food and other goods. Now, Spilhaus thought, a federal commitment and continuing support for sea-related endeavors could bring the United States to a position of leadership in ocean engineering and aquaculture.

Still, despite its glorious reception, Athelstan didn't expect much to become of his cavalier address to the fisheries biologists and managers. But then letters began arriving. Peers called. He was being invited to talk more and at length about the Sea Grant concept. By the end of 1964, Dr. Spilhaus was on a second bona fide lecturing spree. (Remember, he was stumping for the Experimental City during this time, too.)

One of the letters Dr. Spilhaus received was from Saul Saila, professor of oceanography at the Narragansett Marine Laboratory of the University of Rhode Island. He was also one of the heavy hitters that presented at the American Fisheries Society meeting, so when he wrote to Dr. Spilhaus encouraging action on the Sea Grant concept, his opinion had a bit of weight.

Responding, Spilhaus wrote a letter to the president of the University of Rhode Island suggesting that "the Ocean State" could pioneer the Sea Grant concept. He sent a copy of this letter to John Knauss, then the dean of the University of Rhode Island's graduate school of oceanography.

Intrigued and enthusiastic, Knauss shared the idea of a Sea Grant College with Rhode Island's Senator Claiborne Pell. Hearing about the Sea Grant concept so circuitously didn't diminish Pell's interest. He championed it among his colleagues on Capitol Hill.

The defining conference, The Concept of a Sea-Grant University, held October 28 and 29, 1965, was organized by Knauss and co-sponsored by the University of Rhode Island and the Southern New England Marine Sciences Association. Spilhaus again gave a keynote address, which he had polished considerably. Now outlining more specifics, it was still hyperbolic but even more persuasive.

Afterward, Knauss extolled the unique way Sea Grant was conceptualized as an assault on problems of the sea using intellectual resources. The 224 participants were concerned about how the funds might be divvied up, but Knauss countered, "The excitement generated by these ideas will long be remembered."

By this time, Athelstan was convinced that feats of engineering, encouraged by Sea Grant support, would allow humans to build and inhabit sea cities. In addition to improving U.S. fisheries, occu-

From left, Spilhaus, John Knauss, and Senator Claiborne Pell in the foyer of the Viking Hotel, Newport, Rhode Island, 1965. Photo courtesy of Rhode Island Sea Grant.

pancy was one of his primary points. He frequently repeated versions of his 1965 conference address: "Like a military operation where a war is not won until the area is occupied, we will master the sea only when we occupy it," he would say, and add: "Once people can work and live at a thousand feet, the whole of the continental shelf, an area of ten million square miles is opened up as a new continent for our use. Oil drilling, mining, salvage and even fish farming can be done by people down there not, as now, on the end of the string from a wobbly surface."

But Spilhaus's verbal flights of fancy also acknowledged the baggage of reality, the left-brain understanding that "ocean engineering problems are special and unique." Still, he always framed those problems as solvable. "When you occupy a place, whether it be an enemy country, uninhabited polar or desert wastes, the moon, the planets, or the depths of the sea, essentially you have to start worrying about the five basic things for people to live: a way to get there and back; shelter while they are there; power, water, and food." He was quick to note that "materials behave quite differently at the seven-ton-per-square-inch pressures encountered in the abyss." He pointed out that ocean structures need to withstand marine borers and other organisms, as well as catastrophic forces like earthquakes, currents, wave forces, and underwater landslides. And if he had his way, solving those deepwater engineering challenges would start soon.

Before fiscal and political realities reigned in the galloping concept, Sea Grant Colleges were grandly envisioned as institutions that would concentrate on applying science to the sea in ways such as prospecting underwater, mining, developing food resources, discovering marine pharmacology and medicine, improving maritime efficiency and navigation, and manipulating weather and climate. Spilhaus, the futurist author behind *Our New Age* comics, also promoted the Sea Grant idea through these Sunday newspaper strips with speculations about the advantages of fish farming and cultivating sea vegetables. "The harvesting and husbandry of the food we take from the sea is utterly primitive and has not in any sense kept pace with the magnificent progress in fertilizers, farm machinery, cross-breeding and hybridizing that has developed on the land," he said at the 1965 symposium.

Among other imaginative projects, Dr. Spilhaus proposed using porpoises as seagoing sheep dogs, training them to herd fish into nets.

Beyond practical advances, Spilhaus and his supporters wanted Sea Grant institutions to relate applied sea science to underlying natural sciences and to economics, sociology, psychology, politics, and law, as they relate to the occupation of the sea. As they were conceived, Sea Grant colleges were also to incorporate the liberal arts—literature, art, and history—to describe and enhance humanity's relation to our mostly ocean-blue planet.

So, between 1963 and 1966—while he was still stumping for the MCX to a somewhat different audience—the energetic professor was also drumming up enthusiasm for a national Sea Grant Program. He wrote a plethora of letters and articles, and delivered an exhausting number of speeches. His guest editorial in *Science*,

September 4, 1964, became a spark plug. It framed the exciting opportunities and challenges a Sea Grant Program could address in a language that non-scientists could embrace. It referenced a historical precedent, too: "Basic funds, undesignated except that they be used by sea-grant colleges, could be obtained in much the way that agricultural support has been obtained in the past. Establishment of the land-grant colleges was one of the best investments this nation ever made. The same kind of imagination and foresight should be applied to exploitation of the sea."

Later he wrote, "I wanted an EXACT parallel with land grant colleges and I wanted the colleges who participated—the institutions that participated—to be given, in perpetuity, reserved bits of the seashore and waters out to the territorial limits, not only for the experiments . . . but also for the purpose of conserving these areas from excessive exploitation and fouling." But given the cost and legal challenges of granting ocean floor access to research institutions, this idea was necessarily tabled.

Meanwhile in his speeches, Spilhaus was spreading his ideas about controlling the ocean, creating longer coastlines, colonizing the sea, and hybridizing sea plants to produce sea fruits and vegetables. The notion was that Sea Grant's applied research could spin these ideas into reality—these ideas and more, including:

- Farming whales and fish
- Heating ocean waters for recreation and increased fish harvest
- Revitalizing beaches
- Desalinizing seawater to make it potable through biotechnology
- Mining the ocean floors for minerals and metals

Those caught up in the Sea Grant momentum included senators like Edward Kennedy (D-Massachusetts), representatives like Paul

Rogers (D-Florida), and entrepreneurs like Wilbert "Wib" Chapman, director of the Division of Resources of Van Camp Sea Food Company. Senator Warren Magnuson (D-Washington) suggested that legislation to establish Sea Grant Colleges would be more palatable if it included the Great Lakes states—further broadening its appeal. The idea was quickly gaining purchase.

Timing helped tremendously. After the Soviet Union launched Sputnik in 1957, the United States had become competitively and acutely interested in scientific and technological advances. President Kennedy's vow to have an American on the moon by 1970 provided enough intellectual fervor for scientific achievements that the public was receptive to exploring the world's oceans as well as outer space. Indeed, Spilhaus was fond of quipping, "Why do we know less about the ocean's bottom than we do the moon's backside?"

"What we wanted in those early years," said Spilhaus, "was nothing quite so romantic as a man on the moon. It was something infinitely more practical: drawing the resource out of academic institutions and pragmatically putting it to work, in the case of Land Grant, on the farms, in the case of Sea Grant, through a corps of county agents in hip boots."

One of the most important outcomes of the 1965 conference was the National Committee on Sea-Grant Colleges. This committee of university representatives worked to ensure that universities would help shape and promote Sea Grant legislation, garnering both public and professional support. To be designated a Sea Grant College, Dr. Spilhaus thought universities should demonstrate a commitment to the sea. To ensure that they wouldn't use the program as a federal handout, he included a matching fund requirement in the bill: a Sea Grant College needed to match every two federal dollars with one dollar from its own coffers. This match requirement still applies today.

Sea Grant
Becomes a Reality

Might I say just one thing. I think Dr. Spilhaus's address
this morning was one of the most exciting addresses I have
ever heard in my life. —**Francis Horn**, president of the
University of Rhode Island, at the Sea Grant Hearings, 1966

Less than three years after Spilhaus's extemporaneous speech in
Minneapolis, Senate hearings on Sea Grant took place from the
second to the fifth of May 1966, thanks to Claiborne Pell. Debates
over what agency should oversee Sea Grant, and about the allo-
cation of funding, dominated the discussion. The Smithsonian
Institution, the National Science Foundation, and the Department of the Interior were the three top contenders for managing
Sea Grant. The National Science Foundation won round one, and
ended up as Sea Grant's administrator for the new program's first
four years.

"One thing that struck me," said Robert Abel, "was the con-
certed drive to carve up Senator Pell's poor little chicken before
it had even emerged from the shell." Abel was then executive secretary of the Interagency Committee on Oceanography and soon
would serve as the National Sea Grant Program's first director.

Within days after the Senate hearings, Pell sought Dr. Spilhaus's
opinion about who he thought should carry the bill in the House.
He recommended Representative Paul Rogers of Florida, who had
seemed supportive during their conversation about Sea Grant years
earlier. The Pell/Rogers team crafted legislation in simple language that included "ocean, coastal, and Great Lakes resources."
President Lyndon Johnson signed the National Sea Grant College
Program Act on October 15, 1966. The act began with these words:

The Congress finds and declares the following:

(1)   The national interest requires a strategy to—
  (A) provide for the understanding and wise use of ocean,
       coastal, and Great Lakes resources and the environment;
  (B) foster economic competitiveness;
  (C) promote public stewardship and wise economic
       development of the coastal ocean and its margins, the
       Great Lakes, and the exclusive economic zone;
  (D) encourage the development of preparation, forecast,
       analysis, mitigation, response, and recovery systems for
       coastal hazards;
  (E) understand global environmental processes and their
       impacts on ocean, coastal, and Great Lakes resources; and
  (F) promote domestic and international cooperative solutions
       to ocean, coastal, and Great Lakes issues.

The act that passed was a limited version of the vision. Falling far short of Dr. Spilhaus's grand schemes, it provided $1 million to encourage existing institutions to direct their programs toward ocean technology. Still, the act was startling in its alacrity. The speed with which Sea Grant, a complicated program, moved from a spoken idea to reality—three years and thirty-three days—is still considered a record for accomplishment in Washington, DC. Many attribute this fact as much to Spilhaus's eloquent campaigning as to the soundness of the Sea Grant proposal.

Robert Abel, the program's first national director, also noted that the bill contained wording that was "more permissive than any other legislation passed in that era." Why? Perhaps because the National Science Foundation let Abel assemble a panel that included Spilhaus and that NOAA's associate administrator John Townsend Jr. described as "the most murderous and competent cutthroats of any advisory board in Washington."

Spilhaus stumping for
the National Sea Grant
Program, circa 1965.
Photo courtesy of the
Dolph Briscoe Center
for American History,
University of Texas at
Austin.

Senator Pell said, "During the course of the program, I had many opportunities to confer with Dr. Spilhaus. He never hesitated to offer his wisdom, experience and extraordinary imagination to the cause. He also served on the National Sea Grant Advisory Panel. It is impossible to overstate his value to us during those days of designing and operating the national program."

Athelstan had "a tremendous ability to coin a phrase," commented Dr. Knauss in retrospect. "He could capture an essence in a phrase." Knauss did not think Spilhaus was the easiest person to work with, although "I agreed with him more than I disagreed," he later said. "He did not have much tolerance for fuzzy ideas or negotiating or trying to reach some kind of consensus. He was impatient, even with bright men who were discussing matters."

Spilhaus must have been pleased with Sea Grant's success, but frustrated by its limitations. Certainly, Sea Grant generates and serves coastal science to the public. It creates synergy among government, industry, and academia with ocean and Great Lakes interests. But, for example, nothing came of Spilhaus's vision of universities owning patches of ocean floor for researching mineral and deep-sea mining.

The whittling away of Sea Grant's original scope was a disappointing aspect of the program's early development to Athelstan Spilhaus and others. During the program's first ten years, Dr. Spilhaus's visions of ocean engineering weren't materializing and technological advances were minimal, a consequence (at least in part) of funding constraints. When President Nixon created the National Oceanic and Atmospheric Administration (NOAA) in 1970, Sea Grant was one of the programs that found itself shaded by the new and very large NOAA umbrella. However, as the only division of NOAA partnering with universities at the time, Sea Grant was decidedly on the fringe.

On the other hand, the two scientists and two politicians who pulled and pushed Sea Grant into existence—Athelstan Spilhaus, John Knauss, Claiborne Pell, and Paul Rogers—had much to be pleased about on Sea Grant's tenth anniversary. On that occasion, Spilhaus spoke about the definition of economics: "the stewardship of resources with a view to productivity." He said translating that definition to the oceans described Sea Grant's purpose. "It's exactly what NOAA is chartered to do," he said.

Colorful, sharp-thinking, highly innovative, and intensely productive, Dr. Athelstan Spilhaus was, according to many, "the father of Sea Grant." At times he considered himself its mother and Senator Pell its father. To Louise O'Connor, his biographer, he said, "They say I was helpful with Sea Grant. I invented the bloody thing."

Despite his uncanny knack for predicting the future, Dr. Spilhaus had no premonition that his off-the-cuff speech in 1963 would result in a network of over thirty Sea Grant programs conducting research, outreach, and education relating to coastal environments and economies. Sea Grant involves science; it involves law; and it involves society. "Inventing," he wrote later, "is often copying in a new context at the [right] psychological moment."

The National Science Foundation set up the National Sea Grant Office in 1967, which awarded the first Sea Grant grants a year later. By 1971 four institutions became Sea Grant College Programs: Oregon State University, the University of Rhode Island, Texas A & M University, and the University of Washington. The next year the University of Hawaii and the University of Wisconsin also became Sea Grant College Programs based on their record of research and outreach.

Ever energy conscious and ever a visionary, Spilhaus was pleased that Wisconsin Sea Grant was investigating transportation issues. While he was welcoming the University to the program in 1972, he said, "I was interested in your studies of transport and containerization, as related to seaboard ports versus the Great Lakes ports, and the competition with unit trains over land. I think this is healthy because in the future, as we look toward the proper use of energy, we are going to have to examine pretty carefully ways of transportation that are cheaper than the airplane and automobile, which use orders of magnitude more energy per pound than do railroads, pipelines, or ships."

During the same speech, he contemplated the dilemmas of managing invasive species in the Great Lakes. Later, he remembered his father eating lampreys in Poland and the Baltic states, where they are a delicacy. Why not make sea lamprey into a fancy gourmet paté that would fetch a handsome price? He told his audience that the paté could become popular enough to flip the tables—making the invasive sea lamprey an "endangered species" in the Great Lakes. "We'd have the 'ecomaniacs' and other conservationists on our necks," he mused.

In 1998 the Minnesota Sea Grant Program explored the possibility of sending Great Lakes sea lamprey to European dinner plates. With support from the Great Lakes Protection Fund, they found that Great Lakes sea lamprey, whether alive or frozen, *would* be eagerly consumed in Europe, especially in Portugal, *if* the mercury levels in their snaky bodies didn't surpass the European Union standard of 0.3 parts per million—which they did, by a long shot. Even if the EU standard could be met, the conclusion in 1998 was that harvesting and exporting Great Lakes sea lamprey would have been difficult, not because of a shortage of commercial fishermen or lamprey, but because of existing control programs, regulations, and special interests in the United States and Canada. As an inventor, experimenter, and entrepreneur, Dr. Spilhaus often became disgusted over how environmental laws and Food and Drug Administration restrictions hobbled some of what he considered his best ideas.

In his more reflective moods, Spilhaus was pleased with the way the Sea Grant concept gained momentum and what it was during his lifetime. "I think it's exceeded my expectations," he said. He thought Sea Grant's greatest accomplishment was elevating an awareness of the sea. "What I enjoy most is the thousands of students who have been helped by the program, which is a training field for people who deal with the ocean. Sea Grant succeeded very well in that," he said.

However, as an octogenarian he was still known to gripe, "Our fishing efforts are minuscule compared to other countries. . . . [Sea Grant] hasn't done as well in the proper utilization of the sea. It seems to me all the United States uses the sea for is recreation, which is a perfectly good use, but not the sole use."

The Sea Grant model of applied research, extension, and education has now traveled to countries in Latin America, Southeast Asia, and North Africa. Looking to America's National Sea Grant College Program for inspiration, institutions around the world have also become dedicated to applying science and technology to sustainably develop and conserve coastal and marine resources.

6

MOMENTUM TOWARD TOMORROW, 1966–1978

U Dean Spilhaus Will Be "Gadfly"
—Headline, **St. Paul Pioneer Press**, 1966

The fifty-four-year-old Dr. Spilhaus stepped down as dean of the Institute of Technology at the University of Minnesota in 1966, having evolved from a research scientist to a public spokesperson for technology, experimental cities, and Sea Grant. A short item in the *St. Paul Pioneer Press* on June 12 of that year indicated that he resigned "to become a sort of scientific gadfly." In the same article, the university's president, Owen Meredith "Met" Wilson, was cited as telling the board of regents that Spilhaus was one of the most exciting minds around and that he would become an agent provocateur for science. The article went on to say, "The colorful, quotable, and oft-times controversial dean will remain as a professor of physics at the University, but it seems his professorship will be unusual."

Unusual it was. Within fourteen months Wilson was publicly chiding Spilhaus for describing the university as "a great gray mediocrity." Spilhaus made it known that he thought the university was not living up to its potential at about the time he was leaving it in a seeming huff. Later, Spilhaus would admit that his timing was poor.

Rumors, and a few newspaper clips, suggest that Spilhaus was piqued because two men were made president of the University of Minnesota instead of himself: first Wilson in 1960 and then Malcolm Moos in 1967. Letters in Spilhaus's files at the university indicate that some thought the board of regents made a mistake in 1959 when they elected Met Wilson as president; his views on education were diametrically opposed to Athelstan's. Whereas Spilhaus, trained with classical European curricula in engineering and science, favored teaching the fundamentals, Wilson, grounded in history and education through a Mormon lens, tended toward progressive pedagogy. And if, in 1966, Spilhaus had indeed anticipated presiding over the entire University of Minnesota, not just its sizable Institute of Technology, his ego apparently didn't let him stay after being passed over.

A Brief and Bad Move

I am making no apologies for myself, but most things
written about this are very, very slanted. —**Athelstan Spilhaus**

Rather than stay at the university, Dr. Spilhaus accepted the position of president of the Franklin Institute in Philadelphia, one of the oldest and premier centers of science education and development in the United States. An undated newspaper article printed in Philadelphia gushed, "It is hard to imagine a scientist better qualified to serve as president of the Franklin Institute than Dr. Athelstan Spilhaus. He is a scientist, inventor, engineer, research specialist, and authority on both oceanography and space. He has performed outstanding services in each of those fields and perhaps most important of all, has displayed a remarkable talent for communicating his enthusiasm and knowledge to others, young and old, laymen as well as experts."

The effusive welcome to Pennsylvania given to Athelstan and Gail didn't last long. Spilhaus was a cantankerous and controversial figure throughout his career, and he especially became stubborn at the Franklin Institute. He was hired and fired within eighteen months. "The firing briefly masqueraded as a resignation but there were simply too many bloodstains for that story to endure," said Louise O'Connor. Evidently he spent too much time pursuing his own interests for the executive board's tastes. The board suggested that Spilhaus was in business for himself, not the institute, and noted that he refused to be involved in fundraising, the primary task expected of him. Anti-Spilhaus sentiments included a 1968 newspaper article titled "The Curmudgeon of the Comics," in which a peer asserted, "The forbearance of a saint was needed to live with Spilhaus."

Spilhaus was frustrated due to his "inability to bring the institute into the last half of the twentieth century." He said, "My first impression was that the Franklin Institute would be like the World's Fair, and I'd be able to play with all the toys. It was very enjoyable, to be sure, but very different from the World's Fair. I didn't have ten million dollars to put on a show for six months." He thought his drive to modernize education and research was often hobbled by a board lacking in vision. Board members were frustrated, too—and scared. Not only was their director uninterested in raising much-needed money, but he also involved the institute in an unprecedented number of educational, scientific, and community service projects.

From Spilhaus's perspective, he thought other people should be engaged in fundraising and that his expertise as a science communicator should be honored. This year and a half of Athelstan's life was likely his most unfulfilling. He claimed he "couldn't stand" the chairman of the board, Wynn LePage. Spilhaus was not shy about explaining his feelings about LePage to O'Connor, "Everything I

did was blocked by this little man—a complete egotist." Among
other things, Spilhaus objected to the way LePage claimed to work
for the institute for no money and to the way he insisted on being
addressed as "Dr." based on an honorary degree awarded to him
by Lehigh University in 1962.

In addition to disliking his boss, Spilhaus wanted to continue
writing the *Our New Age* cartoon strip and working on experimental
cities. Evidently his interests in developing an experimental city for
Philadelphia had the mayor and city council in a stew. During this
turbulent time, Spilhaus was also elected president of the American
Association for the Advancement of Science, a position and organization that better suited his temperament and skills.

Reflecting on his brother's tribulations, Muir Spilhaus later
wrote to Louise O'Connor:

> [Athelstan] has always seemed to me to be years ahead of his
> time. I have increasingly felt that his absolute genius has basically
> been the cause of his becoming, from time to time, a somewhat con-
> troversial scientist. Apart from that, he has the capacity of whole-
> hearted enjoyment with unreserved and spontaneous expression.
> Our only too rare times together have been highlighted by possibly
> (according to some) rather immoderate celebration.
>
> However, one is often reminded of the fact—when thinking of
> Athel's very hearty enjoyment—that a great many of the world's
> most famous intellectuals have really enjoyed periods of social unac-
> ceptability because of their ruthless truthfulness—their willingness
> to express themselves utterly honestly and forcibly—and "let them-
> selves go," and cease to conform to the regimen of a ordinary society.
>
> The pendulum swings, his personal life has not been free of mis-
> ery, sadness and unhappiness and I have often wondered how he
> has managed to be just himself during these difficult periods.
>
> Physically and mentally he is strong and courageous and his
> forthrightness must produce an "aloneness" at times, but I think he

has always been able to get out of himself by his capacity to utilize his most uncommon intellectual powers by absorbing himself (also "immoderately") in his work, and giving free rein to the unusual mental gifts with which he has been endowed.

Spilhaus commented about his brief tenure at the Franklin Institute: "I was everywhere and an internationally known person. It should have been a feather in their cap but they were too little. They tried to make me into a flunky."

In his opinion, "The stupid, little, small-minded institute would accept no ideas. They had sold ancient artifacts before I got there. It wasn't a public auction—those there got first choice. It was almost a criminal operation."

If Spilhaus had analyzed the recent history of the Franklin Institute or gotten to know its board president, Wynn LePage, before he moved to Pennsylvania, he might have reconsidered the job offer. At a minimum he might have understood that such venerable institutions tend to be tightly controlled by conservative representatives of enduring lineages and companies. Athelstan's modus operandi could not have been further from what the Franklin Institute's executive board expected.

The Sunshine State

I make light of it now but really it was a tough business.
I had to have my phones disconnected because of the numerous
hate calls that came in. —**Athelstan Spilhaus**, on supervising
the desegregation of a Florida school district

After Athel "resigned" from the institute in 1969, the Spilhauses sold their Philadelphia digs and moved to Palm Beach, Florida. Not one to remain idle, Dr. Spilhaus quickly made a bid to become Congressman Spilhaus by arranging to be a contender in the GOP primary of 1970. According to an article in the *Palm Beach Post*, to be eligible "he filed suit testing Florida's five-year residency requirements for public office in Federal court and won."

His campaign platform was based on scientific solutions to national challenges and included—no surprise—solving pollution problems, providing relief for congested cities, and capitalizing on the usefulness of oceans. Suspiciously, his congressional ambitions would have pitted him against his former Sea Grant ally, Democrat Paul Rogers. When Spilhaus withdrew from the race, he "set off a flurry of political rumors, including one that his prominence had been used to scare off other Republican contenders" so that it would be easier for Rogers to retain his seat.

Athelstan withdrew from the race in a telegraph sent from South Africa, where he and his wife, Gail, were visiting his mother. (His father had passed away in 1968.) The journey took some time, maybe more than he had originally intended, for in addition to spending time with family, he was traveling with a "special passport" to conduct touchy business related to refugee camps in the turbulent Middle East. Some suggest that the business was for the CIA; others suggest it was for a nongovernmental organization. Either way, Lebanon, where the Spilhauses found themselves during that time, was a fierce battleground for the conflict that precipitated the Cairo Agreement of 1969.

Upon returning from their harrowing travels, Florida governor Claude Kirk tapped Athelstan to serve, temporarily, as a school superintendent to help peacefully desegregate a then racially divided Palm Beach County. Dr. Spilhaus's qualifications included a knowledgeable perspective on race, which reflected his South

African heritage, and his administrative experience in academia. However, Spilhaus reportedly asked, "Claude, when you asked me to do this, were you basing it on my credentials as an educator, or on my experience in guerrilla warfare in China?" He said Governor Kirk replied, "Possibly a mixture of both."

In keeping with his character, Spilhaus managed to generate a series of brouhahas in the short three months he served as superintendent beginning on August 23, 1970. He made news headlines by eating in the school cafeteria and declaring he liked it. He was involved in disputes about bilingualism (against it), forced busing (for it), dress codes (against them, to a point), discipline (for it), and redistricting (for it).

His job included meshing the "Gold Coast" students (Palm Beach) with what he called the "Cliff of Poverty" inland students (West Palm Beach and Fort Lauderdale). Overcoming economic, racial, educational, and language barriers, Spilhaus managed to start the 1970 school year with surprising ease. Part of his success stemmed from the way he reassigned popular band and athletic teachers to new levels of authority and to different schools.

Dr. Spilhaus publicly resigned as superintendent at a press conference held in his home ten days before his fifty-ninth birthday, leaving the job open for the former superintendent, whom the Florida courts exonerated of "malfeasance and misfeasance"—the reasons they replaced him with Athel.

"I thought I could continue with various projects by operating out of the Palm Beach home," said Spilhaus. "But it was soon obvious that this decision was a mistake." The pursuits that Dr. Spilhaus thought would keep him interested didn't. "Palm Beach, intellectually, was an absolute desert," he said. "I found I was flying often to Washington to get somebody to talk to. . . . The idea of working in a physically perfect place, where I have to laze around and all my neighbors are doing absolutely nothing, is the most mentally enervating kind of thing imaginable."

Spilhaus claims ennui was setting in until the famous American architect Wallace Harrison called. Harrison had visited the World's Fair in Seattle, and although he hadn't met Spilhaus, he left the fair with a deep enough impression of Spilhaus's work to ask him if he was interested in helping to design a sunken plaza for Rockefeller Center in New York City. Spilhaus jumped at the assignment. His mandate was to create an interesting public space with a scientific twist outside the McGraw-Hill Building. Thus an artist and the "Plaza of the Solar System" were born.

The Day Earth Was Stolen

What a lovely way to learn geography.
—**Athelstan Spilhaus**, public artist

Spilhaus developed the solar system concept and selected the materials with help from the architectural firm Harrison and Abramovitz, which designed the McGraw-Hill Building. "My idea in this kind of outdoor sculpture is that it is 'Designed by Nature—Interpreted by Spilhaus,'" said the inventor-turned-academician-turned-artist.

The focal point of the Plaza of the Solar System, erected in 1973 at 1221 Avenue of the Americas, remains to this day: the *Sun Triangle*, also referred to as the *Solar Triangle*. The fifty-foot stainless steel isosceles triangle towers above the pavement. Its mirrored surface reflects the pattern of the surrounding skyscrapers, but more importantly, the triangle marks the positions of the sun in the sky at the solstices and equinoxes. The steepest side points to the sun's locale at about noon on June 21, and the lowest side points to its position at about noon on December 21. The third side, the longest one, points to the sun's positions, at the cusps, of spring in March and autumn in September.

Sun Triangle, the focal point of the Plaza of the Solar System, and Spilhaus's map mosaics, remain. Photo by Paul Facazio, New York Sea Grant; sketch by Russell Habermann, Minnesota Sea Grant.

Photo by Jim Henderson, made available under Creative Commons CC0 1.0 Universal Public Domain Dedication.

Nearby, a pool represented the sun. It could be lit, and its swirling water gave the illusion of sunspots. The pool was edged with mirrored stainless steel spheres representing the planets, scaled in proportion to the thirty-foot-diameter "sun" pool. They were not scaled to distance, however. If they were, little Pluto—a planet in 1973—would have been miles away. (The pool was later removed.)

Two of Spilhaus's original map projections remain embedded in the pavement. These mosaics show the "world ocean" and the "world continent." Bronze strips outlining the continents separated colored areas of terrazzo. Spilhaus called them "macro-terrazzo-cloisonné." Embedded stainless steel marked lines of latitude and longitude within these sizable renditions of Earth.

Spilhaus loved the project and loved even more the way people interacted with it. He recounted that one day he received a frantic call from McGraw-Hill saying somebody had stolen Earth, which was about the size of a baseball. When the company asked what they should do about it, Spilhaus answered, "Pay the money to replace it, and put in a bigger stanchion. After all, you can charge it off to publicity. It's the first instance of cosmic larceny." Spilhaus said that they "laughed like hell and replaced it."

He delighted in the way people were learning about their Earth and solar system through his plaza. Youngsters would stand on the maps and say things like "I'll push you into the Pacific Ocean" and "I'll shove you off Greenland!"

Spilhaus also designed a plaza in Elmira, New York, with a similar isosceles triangle that remains to this day. "The triangle is an eternal one, so that it can be put anywhere in the world and just tilted differently according to latitude," he said. Only the inclination of the longest side to the horizon needed to change in order for the other legs of the triangle to stretch toward the Tropic of Cancer and the Tropic of Capricorn, about 23 degrees, 26 minutes.

During this public sculpture period of his life, Spilhaus also fabricated a working model of an environmental sculpture he called a "global solar-lunar dial." It extended the concept of a traditional sundial by showing the progression of the sun between the tropics on the inside of a dome.

After pursuing politics and school administration in Florida, and while emerging as an artist in 1971, Athelstan moved to Washington, DC, with his wife, Gail. The move was precipitated by Athel's appointment as one of the first fellows at the newly minted Woodrow Wilson International Center for Scholars, a place where academics and public servants worked together on major challenges. "The Center gave me a very nice, understandable reason to leave Florida," he said. "I thoroughly enjoyed my time there. The fellows always got together routinely at noon for a drop of sherry and an informal conversation. Perhaps one would talk about what he was working on. There were good people and it was a great place."

Athelstan happily resumed his place in the limelight, traveling extensively to deliver speeches and enliven board meetings, including the board of the American Association for the Advancement of Science (AAAS), which he continued to chair. Wielding his notorious sharp tongue, effervescence, and quick wit, Spilhaus thought and talked extensively about innovative ideas such as using energy as a unit of currency. He spoke about sustainability, oceanography, meteorology, technology, and "ecolibrium," his moniker for balancing ecology and economy. He struggled with the political aspects of science organizations like AAAS and social climbing in general, which he claimed were overtly displayed in Washington.

As much as the Spilhauses enjoyed being DC movers and shakers, they still hadn't found their Eden. Their hectic pace eventually pushed them to seek a retreat from the rat race. They found one in Middleburg, Virginia, fifty miles away, where they bought an eight-acre property with an eighteenth-century stone house and room for horses. By the time Athelstan completed his three years at the Woodrow Wilson International Center in 1974, the Spilhauses were full residents of Middleburg.

"We both loved our place and the small town so much that we found ourselves spending less and less time in our Washington townhouse," said Athelstan. He made this claim despite the Civil War ghost that apparently haunted the old well during full moons.

Following Athelstan's work to solve some of the world's deepest problems at the Wilson Center, Robert White, the administrator of the National Oceanic and Atmospheric Administration, offered Spilhaus the chief scientist position at the agency.

Spilhaus was reluctant to accept. It would have been another presidential appointment involving copious mounds of bureaucratic paperwork. As an alternative, White convinced Spilhaus to become his special assistant for three days a week. This part-time NOAA gig seemed to give Spilhaus, who was sixty-three, a second wind. He kept the advisory position with NOAA from 1974 until 1980. Spilhaus enjoyed the arrangement because, as he said, "I had lots of other things to do, including the sculpture that was ongoing."

Around this period of his life he mused, "I'm trying to find out who is steering science. Some feel that science cannot be steered and that the scientist should stay in his lab and find out how things tick. I'm very concerned at looking at science not as a thing of itself, but as a part of our total culture, just as painting, music, and literature [are]."

Consulting with NOAA kept Dr. Spilhaus at his city office in Georgetown from Tuesday through Thursday each week. He spent the intervening nights at the members-only Cosmos Club, a few blocks away. He said, "This left Gail alone in Middleburg. Again, I was making the same damn mistake I'd made before. I hadn't learned from past experience, so I set the stage for tragedy."

While Athelstan worked in the city and traveled to attend meetings and to deliver the galvanizing speeches he was famous for, Gail maintained the Virginia homestead, which included horses, two standard poodles, and too much alcohol. She died of a perforated ulcer in 1978 while Athelstan was lecturing at a World Business Council meeting in New Mexico.

"After Gail died, I couldn't stand the look of the place we both loved so much, so I accepted a visiting professorship at the University of Texas in Austin," he said. "I was sick in mind and body. I had been through a lung resection the previous December and was recovering from tuberculosis."

Spilhaus's stay in Austin was brief. The man he traveled west to work with, Creighton Burk, had joined the faculty of the University of Texas a few years earlier, having been the chief geologist of Mobil Oil Corporation and an adjunct professor at Princeton. Shockingly, the forty-nine-year-old petroleum geologist and head of the university's Marine Science Institute had a massive disabling stroke just before Athelstan arrived. Distressed and lonely, Spilhaus channeled his grief into ideas about seaward expansion and the details of underwater living; he also helped keep the Marine Science Institute operating in Port Aransas and the Virgin Islands. By the end of 1978, he returned to his ghost-filled home in Middleburg.

7

LEAVING THE WORLD IN BETTER SHAPE, 1979–1998

As an ocean person, I would say slice the lands
instead of the oceans. —**Athelstan Spilhaus** on world maps,
as told to Walter Cronkite, 1982

A thelstan readily admitted that he "was hopeless at living alone." Within four months of meeting Kathleen Fitzgerald in 1979, Athel was standing before a justice of the peace in paint-spattered jeans saying, "I do." Their courtship was practically nonexistent, and their nuptials were impromptu.

As Kathy remembered it, she met Athel during a shipboard science workshop for teachers. At forty-one, she was a single mother; he was her sixty-seven-year-old instructor. She was sassy and curious; he was riveting and irreverent. During the course of the workshop cruise they discovered they lived only about a valley apart in the rolling hills of Virginia. After returning to land, they visited each other and became friendly enough that when Athel asked her, Kathy agreed to drive him to the Washington Dulles International Airport one day.

On the way to the airport, Kathy asked her older friend about his trip. He said he was flying out to Seattle to ask a woman he knew to marry him. She responded, "What about me?" He said, "Turn the car around."

"That was a Wednesday," she said. "We talked all night and got married on Thursday." The bride wore denim pants that showed signs of her recent battle to turn grapes into jelly. The groom had recently been painting. "Of course my children thought I had a mental breakdown," she said.

It was a match made in heaven, assuming heavenly sorts of matches include two iron-willed, unorthodox, and "why-the-hell-not" kind of people who are passionate about antique toys and dogs. "They were a great team," said family friend Joe Vadus.

Kathy and her youngest child, who still lived at home, moved into the stone house. Kathy said, "Living with Athel was exciting; we fought all the time!" Her devotion to him was abundantly clear as she recounted stories and pointed out his favorite recipes in an old South African cookbook in a home that had not changed much since Gail had passed away over a decade earlier.

Kathy traveled with Athelstan as his helpmate to numerous conferences and board meetings, which facilitated their mutual and avid interest in collecting mechanical toys. With a twinkle in her eye, Kathy observed, "I always said that Athel could never hold a job."

Kathy and Athel in Guana Cay. Photo courtesy of Kathy Spilhaus.

Reflecting on her husband's approach to his work, Kathy said, "Athel would give you the concept—he didn't want to be bothered with the nuts and bolts of how it is done—the engineers can build it. He had complete confidence that they can carry out his concepts."

As Athelstan put it himself, "My work is to have ideas. It's the only high-level activity of the human brain. I was born with a logical mind and the gift of a phrase, and that gift has prevented pontification and made my scoldings through the years more palatable, I would hope. I guess I could have gone into politics or played piano in a whorehouse, but because the latter, to my way of thinking, is the more honorable of the two professions, and I can't play the piano, I decided to go to engineering school and put my ideas to work."

As his chief assistant, Kathy observed, "For someone who has invented machinery, labor-saving devices and scientific instruments, he is amazingly resistant to using modern machinery himself. He really carries this eccentricity to extremes at times. He hates phones and computers, but he does love the fax. However, he won't use it himself."

While Athel was alive, Kathy ran the household. Athel applied considerable creative energy toward remapping Earth, a collaboration with the Smithsonian Institution. Athel said to Louise O'Connor, whom he had met during his stint in Austin, Texas, "I continue to work as a catalyst and stimulator to my old project of colonizing the oceans." And then he added, "Lately, my comparatively leisurely life in Middleburg has enabled me to concentrate on important things such as my lifelong interest in maps. Misuse of maps has bothered me since childhood."

As a youngster learning about the world from a South African perspective, Athelstan objected that the North Pole was always put at the top of the map. He called it his "first brush with polarized discrimination." Later he became peeved that maps slashed through oceans. Aware that standard Mercator maps were useful for navigation but not for showing the world as it is, he had already begun dabbling in cartography in the early 1940s. Now, starting in 1979, he became diligent about this pursuit.

Four hundred years earlier, in 1569, cartographer Gerardus Mercator had introduced the familiar flat representation of our round planet. Mercator's projection became a nautical sensation because it was gridded with straight lines that shipping concerns could use for navigating the treacherous seas. To achieve a flat map with straight lines depicting a round object, a Mercator projection sacrifices accurate proportions toward the North and South poles. Small landmasses like Iceland are shown relatively accurately, but Mercator maps distort the size and shape of large masses such as Antarctica and Greenland. Dr. Spilhaus's maps evolved from Mercator's.

Spilhaus said, "A world map is a mathematical picture that conveys some essence to the eye. A picture by a great artist is also an abstraction of the essence of what he sees. Both the artists who paint pictures and those we call cartographers distill the three dimensions of the solid world to two on a flat plane. Each time we skin the orange peel that represents our globe and try to flatten out the skin to make a map, we must of necessity distort. But distortion need not be a detriment . . . we choose our distortions to emphasize what we want to see—as an artist may distort for emphasis."

In some ways, Spilhaus's early sentiments and activities regarding world maps echoed those of Buckminster Fuller, who began refiguring maps in 1934. But when Spilhaus became a serious mapmaker in 1979, he gravitated toward crafting "interrupted maps" where the waters and lands were not contained within squares, rectangles, or ovals.

Spilhaus considered cartography a species of art; "geo-art," he called it. Without question some of his mapping became art, like the Infinite Earth picture he produced during his last years. Referencing Picasso's painting of a woman who is both profile and full face, he said the master had only gone halfway. "He only did profile and full face," he said in an interview. "When we do the world on a flat sheet of paper, we do both profiles, full face, and the back of the head . . . on one drawing."

Complementing his blended interests in art and science, Spilhaus had a style of communicating that resonated with people. How did he come up with a map to show connected oceans? He described it this way in a 1979 *Smithsonian Magazine* article:

> The most common way of interrupting the skin [of the Earth] for world maps is to make two pinpricks, at the North and South poles, and a cut joining them through the Pacific Ocean. The skin is then flattened into rectangular or elliptical forms with the poles, with their maximum distortion, at the top and bottom. (In the case of Mercator's map the distortion at the poles is such that they cannot be shown at all.)
>
> But having decided to use two pinpricks, you need not limit yourself to the geographic poles. You can use any two points for poles that are opposite each other. If you pierce a globe with a knitting needle so that the needle passes through the center of the sphere, it will come out at a point exactly opposite its point of entry. These points are called antipodes.
>
> The old children's notion of digging vertically through the Earth (or the new nuclear scare story of melting through) and coming out in China is a misconception. If you dug vertically from any point in the conterminous United States, you would come out in the Indian Ocean. In fact, if the game is played on almost any continent, the result is the same: you surface in an ocean! Only about three percent of the Earth's land is antipodal, or opposite other land.

To emphasize continuous oceans, Spilhaus couldn't use the antipodal North and South Poles, since the North Pole is in the middle of the Arctic Ocean. But to make a flat picture of the world's oceans they would need to be clipped somewhere. He thought that this "somewhere" should be at the narrowest junctions of the three ocean lobes created by "unpeeling" the planet. That spot was the Bering Sea, between Alaska and Siberia. One of the justifications he sometimes used was that the Bering Sea was too shallow and too narrow to constitute "real ocean."

The trouble with maps, Spilhaus told Water Cronkite and his TV viewers in 1982, is that they have to have edges that often interrupt something of interest to some viewer. Spilhaus objected to the way Mercator split the Pacific Ocean and distorted the poles.

Spilhaus understood that a single ocean covers nearly three-quarters of Earth and that maps emphasizing land were next to useless for showing the way winds and currents move. For that matter, whales, too. In 1983 he published the first world map showing oceans the way he truly favored them being shown. He called it "my Ultimate Map of the Oceans."

In his *Atlas of the World with Geophysical Boundaries Showing Oceans, Continents and Tectonic Plates in Their Entirety,* published in 1991 by the American Philosophical Society, Spilhaus created maps with edges that relied on geophysical features like shorelines or tectonic plates. Landmasses were scaled proportionately. And, unsurprisingly, the aspect was chosen to show off some point about our Earth. "Aspect is the choice of what the artist wants the viewer to see," he said. "It is what puts 'art' in c*art*ography." Athelstan finished his mapping of the Earth two days before he died. He told his wife, "The world map is perfected; I have been working on it since 1942."

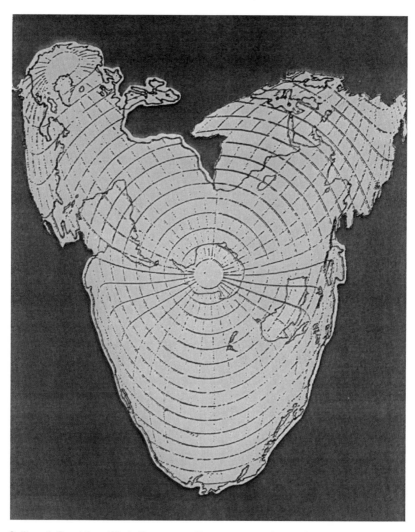

Spilhaus's Equal Area Whole Ocean map. Photo courtesy of Kathy Spilhaus.

8

WORK AND PLAY ARE INDISTINGUISHABLE, 1911–1998

I have always been fortunate enough to be unable
to distinguish between my work and play. —**Athelstan Spilhaus**

Spilhaus's world-class collection of antique mechanical toys might, at first glance, seem like an odd departure from his scientific interests. Far from it. About toys, he said, "I find myself drawn to the wonderful mechanical ones about the size of the human hand. . . . Perhaps the most intriguing are those based on the simplest mechanical principles, which have lasted through the centuries. These toys use gears, wheels, swinging pendulums, gravity, centrifugal force, or balance. . . . Like science fiction, toys can show the shape of things to come, as in the balloons, zeppelins and airplanes made in the nineteenth century."

Before 1965, Athelstan casually picked up toys that piqued his curiosity or interest. But after he married his second wife, Gail, the couple started accumulating so many mechanical toys that when they moved to Middleburg, they built a three-room museum addition to the house. Kathy, too, gamely took up the pursuit when she married Athel. Their collection became the largest private one in the world and attracted toy aficionados from far and wide, including ZZ Top's Billy Gibbons.

Toys gave Dr. Spilhaus yet another topic to think and write about, and finding toys gave purpose to his travels. Spilhaus said, "We live in a world of reality. We have to make our livings in it. Toys can be a marvelous escape to a world of fantasy and they enable us to rediscover the child in ourselves and to retain the childish virtues of wonder, curiosity, play and puzzle solving."

In 1989, Crown Publishing produced Athelstan and Kathy's book, *Mechanical Toys*, in time for Christmas distribution. He believed that although rare and old toys could fetch significant prices, toys are really worth only as much as they are cherished, admired, and played with. By that definition, the Spilhauses' toys were worth a fortune. By accounting definitions, the 4,000 or so functioning antiques were also worth a fortune.

In 1993 the Spilhauses negotiated what Kathy called "the worst custody fight I've seen." It was over toys. They needed to cull about 500 of them from the collection or build yet another climate-controlled addition. Maybe partially explaining his attachments to

One of the approximately 4,000 mechanical toys in Athel and Kathy's collection. Photo by Sharon Moen.

the collection, Athelstan noted that when he was a lad in South Africa, toys were scarce. "I played with mud animals I fashioned along the riverside," he said.

Auctioneer Noel Barrett said, "He didn't always buy toys in the best condition, but he has examples of every mechanism there is." According to many collectors, the Spilhaus collection was unique in its breadth and that nearly all of the toys were assembled before the quality of mechanical toys declined around 1950. "Few modern toys meet our tastes," said Athel. "Old ones combine beauty, humor, art and music. Modern toys lack that."

At age seventy-two, Athelstan began a business along with Kathy and his youngest son, Karl. The purpose of Pan Geo, Inc., was to "engage in research, collection, renovation, construction purchase, sale, trade and all other activities of any nature related to mechanical toys and other scientific and technological instruments and devices." Pan Geo's products included Earth models and map jig-

Athelstan toying with the Geoglyph puzzle he created, circa 1990.
Photo courtesy of Kathy Spilhaus.

saw puzzles. The words emblazoned on the back of the "Spilhaus Geoglyph Puzzle" box aptly reflected Athelstan's humor and sensibilities: "for all who would like to push the world around."

"I have participated in putting up spaceships and satellites," Athelstan said. "I have invented the bathythermograph, which turned out to be very useful in the exploration of the oceans. I have designed my space clock that tells lots of different times and takes lots of time to set, and the comfortmeter that tells you if you are comfortable or not and turns out to be useless, but very amusing. . . . I regard all of these things as toys."

As a testament to his playful spirit and his roots, Athelstan had ceramic tiles made for his bathroom that depicted Rudyard Kipling's illuminated lettering. His spirits were undampened by a bout of colon cancer in the late 1980s; even after he had been surgically "edited"—"They amended my punctuation and changed my colon to a semicolon"—Spilhaus continued to entertain and educate audiences of all sizes with witty speeches.

One of these speeches was later immortalized in a chapter of a recreational math book, *The Lighter Side of Mathematics*. Spilhaus's chapter, "Escheresch," like himself, encompassed art and science. Athelstan was intrigued by the work of Dutch artist Maurits Escher, whose tessellated images might show a variety of creatures interlocking like tiles, geometrically impossible scenes, and other paradoxes. Spilhaus thought that like Escher, he was maybe a bit too intellectual to be classified as a "real artist." To prepare for the "Escheresch" presentation he was to make to the American Philosophical Society, Spilhaus created a prop, a performing toy of sorts. John Ptak, a history-of-ideas blogger and owner of a rare book business, witnessed the making of that toy on January 28, 1986.

Ptak had driven from Georgetown to Middleburg to buy some books from Dr. Spilhaus. Ptak describes it as an extraordinary day for three reasons: It was the day the space shuttle *Challenger* exploded seventy-three seconds after launching. It was the day he stumbled on the world's largest privately owned nineteenth-century mechanical toy collection. And it was the day he witnessed a man perform a feat he still finds astonishing.

"When I drove up at about nine a.m., I noticed the house was odd, having both old structure and new additions," said Ptak. "When I went inside, I couldn't help but comment on about a dozen or so beautiful and old mechanical toys. Athelstan asked, 'Would you like to see more?' Then he took me to a second room, and a third room, and another. Being in the rare book business, I had dealt with many collections and estates; this was something entirely different. It was phenomenal. It was really just unbelievable."

"So was the man," Ptak said. Seeing 3,000 or so working, remarkable, antique toys was only a precursor. "Dr. Spilhaus was an insanely accomplished man—too much, really incredible."

Ptak said that Athelstan, who was then seventy-six years old, wanted to watch the *Challenger* launch, so the television was on. After the fatal explosion, they spent the rest of the day together. As they watched the story unfold, Athelstan talked and tinkered.

"Running the type of shop I did, I was used to talking to a variety of interesting people, but Dr. Spilhaus was something else," said Ptak. "I'd make one statement and he would pick it up and run it in for a touchdown every time. Meanwhile, he had a box of what looked like junk in front of him. He used a little pocketknife to whittle away bits of wood. He had pieces of string, and dowels, and glass. He said he was making something to illustrate a point he wanted to make at a lecture he was going to give to the American Philosophical Society."

Spilhaus's work in progress was on and within the box. It included two opaque panes of Plexiglas, two articulated wooden disks, and a wooden hand. It employed rubber bands and batteries and a grease pencil so that, when all was said and done, the "toy" produced an Escher-like rendition of a hand drawing a hand.

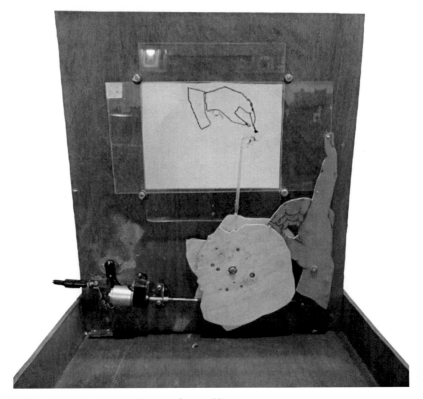

Spilhaus's Escher machine. Photo by Sharon Moen.

"Despite the TV, me, interruptions from his wife, and who knows what else, by the end of the day Athelstan had made this wonderful thing!" said Ptak. "I thought it was phenomenal. I thought it was impossible. I can't imagine creating what he did out of fluff and spit. It really is an example of Athelstan's powerful mind. All things considered—the ephemeral nature of what he was doing, the materials, the interruptions, and so on—I've just never seen anything like it."

Over the next twelve years Athelstan continued speaking at conferences, writing about ocean affairs, collecting toys, and working on maps of the Earth. But he was slowing down. He was a heavy smoker, a habit that caught up with him later in life in the form of chronic bronchitis and emphysema. Finally his health declined to the point where he needed an oxygen tank and a wheelchair, but he still attended the Middleburg races in his 1936 nine-passenger Rolls Royce. And he still engaged in thought-provoking conversations with his friends.

"He was a role model," said longtime friend and colleague Joseph Vadus, a marine engineer who contributed to remote submarines and discovering the sunken Titanic. "His great sense of humor, sharp intellect, and curiosity persisted until his death."

During the night of March 29, 1998, Athelstan Spilhaus died at home in Middleburg, Virginia. According to his wife, Kathy, he probably died of heart failure; she said he had had a pacemaker implanted about two weeks before his passing. His obituary attributed his death to chronic obstructive pulmonary disease.

Impressively active until the end, Dr. Spilhaus held numerous positions upon his death at age eighty-six:

- president: Pan Geo, Inc., National Maritime Center Foundation
- trustee: Aerospace Co.
- director: Science Service Inc., American Dynamics Co., Donaldson Co.
- chairman: Scientific Advisory Committee of the American Newspaper Publishers Association, National Fisheries Center and Aquarium Advisory Board of the U.S. Department of the Interior
- fellow: Royal Meteorological Society, American Geophysical Union, American Association for the Advancement of Science

- board member: Year of the Ocean Foundation
- member: National Academy of Sciences (Committee on Oceanography and Committee on Polar Research), Royal Society of South Africa, American Meteorological Society, American Society of Limnology and Oceanography, American Philosophical Society

Athelstan's ashes were buried in Arlington National Cemetery with full military honors. Well, about half of them were buried there. With help from Louise O'Connor, Kathy Spilhaus scattered about a quarter of the remaining ashes in the Gulf Stream, honoring the importance of his days with Rossby at MIT. She gave the rest to the sea at the twentieth meridian east, where the Indian Ocean meets the Atlantic Ocean off the tip of South Africa.

If there was a question about where Athelstan's heart lay—the atmosphere, the ocean, or the future—the question was answered through his death. In lieu of flowers, the family requested that mourners make contributions to the Woods Hole Oceanographic Institution.

Athelstan's survivors included his wife, Kathleen Ann Fitzgerald Spilhaus; his daughter, Margaret Ann; and his two sons, A. F. Jr. (Fred) and Karl Henry. At the time of his death he had thirteen grandchildren and five great-grandchildren. The family received friends on April 4 at Royston Funeral Home, followed by services at Emmanuel Episcopal Church in Middleburg. Athelstan probably would have best enjoyed the reception at the Cosmos Club in Washington, DC.

The Woods Hole Oceanographic Institution issued a poignant announcement of Athelstan's passing. The overview of this extraordinary man's life began this way:

The Woods Hole Oceanographic Institution announces with great sorrow the death of Honorary Trustee and Member and former employee Dr. Athelstan Frederick Spilhaus during the night of March 29–30, 1998 at his home in Middleburg, Virginia. He was 86. Called by many a Renaissance Man, Dr. Spilhaus is well-known for inventing the bathythermograph (or BT), a temperature measuring device which played a major role in defense against German submarines during World War II, and as the "father" of the Sea Grant College program.

The announcement, elaborating on the outline of his obituary, went on to say:

> His long association with the Institution began in 1934, when as a student of Carl Rossby he started work on a model of a rotating ocean with a jet stream somewhat like the Gulf Stream in it. He accompanied Rossby on a summer cruise that year on R/V Atlantis, helping Rossby with a device called an Oceanograph meant to get continuous tracings of temperature versus depth in the surface layers of the ocean more easily than the standard practice of using a series of reversing thermometers attached to Nansen bottles. The Oceanograph didn't work very well, and Spilhaus thought about it during a year in South Africa. He returned to MIT and began building a better device. Henry Bigelow and Columbus Iselin provided him with some ship time in 1936 and 1937 to test his instrument, and by the summer of 1937 he had a workable device he named the bathythermograph (BT). Its initial application was for biologists and oceanographers, but Iselin saw an application in the detection of submarines in conjunction with sonar. . . .
>
> Spilhaus, who became an Assistant Professor at New York University (NYU) in 1937 while continuing to work summers at WHOI, also aided U.S. forces in World War II. By special act of Congress in 1943, he became a temporary officer in the Army Air Corps although still a British citizen. In 1944 and 1945 he ran weather stations in northern China, living in caves near Mao Tse-Tung's

headquarters behind Japanese lines, supplying weather reports critical to U.S. bombers out of Guam and Saipan. Spilhaus became a U.S. citizen in 1946, and that same year was named Director of Research at NYU. With a knowledge of German, he played a role in bringing German rocket scientists to the U.S. after the war to participate in the Vanguard Program.

In 1948 Spilhaus left NYU to become Dean of the Institute of Technology at the University of Minnesota, a position he held for eighteen years. While at Minnesota he launched a weekly science-oriented comic strip called *Our New Age*, syndicated in more than one hundred newspapers around the world from 1957 to 1973. He also developed the concept of experimental cities with fixed occupancy, waste management, and state of the art communication, adopted in Sweden, Scotland and France. A futurist before the term was created, Spilhaus conceived the idea of covered skyways and tunnels connecting city buildings and allowing easy passage in inclement weather. The concept was first put into practice in Minneapolis in the 1950s.

In 1951 Spilhaus was named Scientific Director of Weapons Effects for two Nevada atomic tests, and the following year became a consultant to the Armed Forces Special Weapons Project under the Department of Defense. He was awarded the Exceptional Civilian Service Medal by the U.S. Air Force in 1952. In 1954 President Dwight Eisenhower appointed Spilhaus the first U.S. Representative to the United Nations Educational, Scientific and Cultural Organization (UNESCO). He served on the Committee on Oceanography of the National Academy of Sciences in 1958–1959. In 1961 President John F. Kennedy appointed him United States Commissioner to the Seattle World's Fair, where he created the U.S. science exhibit, which endures today as the Pacific Science Center. President Lyndon Johnson appointed him to the National Science Board, which he served as a member from 1966 to 1972.

In 1963 Spilhaus called for the establishment of Sea Grant Colleges at a meeting of the American Fisheries Society in Minneapolis; the Sea Grant College Program became a reality a few years later. . . . During the 1970s he served as President of the American Association for the Advancement of Science, as a Fellow of the Woodrow Wilson International Center for Scholars, and was a consultant to the National Oceanic and Atmospheric Administration. He was awarded 11 honorary degrees and received many honors, including the Legion of Merit Award and Sweden's Berzelius Medal.

A man of many talents, Spilhaus was also a sculptor whose work demonstrating geophysical principles is in several cities across the country. To relax, he collected antique mechanical toys. . . . He once said his life could be summed up in one sentence: "Work and play should be indistinguishable."

EPILOGUE

LARGER THAN LIFE

Allyn and Adelaide Vine, Spilhaus's colleagues during his BT days, told Louise O'Connor that in many African religions, it is believed that your spirit does not go to heaven when you die but goes only partway into orbit and stays there as long as anyone who knew you is alive. By this belief system, they suggested that Athelstan would be in orbit for a long time because he'll surely be talked about and remembered well into the future.

Allyn Vine, scientist emeritus with Woods Hole Oceanographic Institution, expressed sympathy for those who did not know Athelstan in his younger days when his energy was unimaginable—to the point where "many people could not stand him." Mr. Vine said, "Scientists tend to be egotistical and mathematicians more so, but whatever profession you are in, it is fun to watch a real pro in your field, and Athel [was] definitely a pro. There are a lot of eccentrics in our business. Athel was at the top of that list, but he was still very practical. He was even practical enough to have made some money in his career."

"He has made a great impression on many people in a positive sense," said Adelaide Vine. "He is one of the major figures in our profession, but it is an obscure profession. If some of his language was crude, it was very effective and understood." She said that, like many who challenge the world, the nervy Dr. Spilhaus was not loved by all. "The forefront is a very rough place," she said.

Athelstan became known as an oceanographer by meteorologists and a meteorologist by oceanographers. Meanwhile, many saw him as an educator or as a scientific administrator. "Dad's greatest contribution may be the comic strip," said Fred Spilhaus. "When you contemplate the number of children he touched with it, who may have later gone into science or simply understood scientific principles better, you realize it had to be a very, very powerful thing. It was an important contribution."

Willard Bascom, a friend and a leader in the early days of deep-sea exploration, said that "[Athel's] greatest achievement was persuading many people that science is fun and that oceanography encompasses many branches of science." Bascom viewed Athel as a person who experimented with ideas. He cited the National Sea Grant Program as an example of a Spilhaus idea that worked out exceptionally well.

While Athelstan was still alive, another friend, Winifred Carter, noted: "Everybody is unique by definition. Athelstan Spilhaus is exceptional in many fields. He has an established reputation in meteorology, marine biology, mechanics, sculpture, antique toys, writing comic strips, developing educational materials relating to geography, inventions such as the bathythermograph and clocks. . . . He may be most known for his outrageous put-downs, his wild beloved imagination, and his lovely ability at story-telling and singing songs! He's also not adverse to minor sins like drinking and smoking and generally enjoying the good things in life."

Dr. Kenneth Spengler, former director of the American Meteorological Society, was quoted as saying, "He has about an idea a week. I would not take any of them lightly. . . . He likes to shake people up and dramatize things. But he is a sound scientist. He's such a diversified fellow. He pops up everywhere."

In the same article, Dr. Robert White said, "He is a futurist, a man who is always thinking about 20 years ahead—at least 20 years ahead. And sometimes it takes quite a bit of time before we all catch up."

In that article Dr. Spilhaus countered, "I am not really much of a futurist. I like to look ahead pragmatically and realistically. . . . I say I'm willing to look ahead for one 'granny.'" (A 'granny' means you can plan realistically for your grandchildren's lives—a hundred years or so.) "The others speculate about the extinction of the sun and everything like that. They're having fun. But from a practical planning point of view for people, I think a granny's a pretty good unit."

Kathy Spilhaus, who died in a car accident in 2011, thought that the world missed the fact that her husband was actually shy and unsure of himself. She said Athel worried about putting forth his best effort, not because he cared about what people thought about him but because he cared that he would be able to live up to what the world expected of him. Whether a blessing or a curse, there is no doubt that Dr. Spilhaus was brutally intelligent and amazingly active.

"Athelstan was seldom without an idea, an opinion, or at least a suggestion," said Louise O'Connor. "Athelstan told me that he had no real life plan except to watch for or make opportunities to do something interesting and different. Athel said that he wanted to run things, not because he enjoyed running them, but because he thought he could run them better. It was difficult for Athel to work for anyone else."

If Athelstan were alive today, he would surely have something to say about climate change. He certainly did while he was living. "The thermostat of the world is the oceans," he said. "One of the water's unique properties is its heat storage capacity." Spilhaus imagined people would eventually master climate in a way that would allow them to artificially create rain and redirect the intense energy of hurricanes. As Wildermuth aptly suggested, Spilhaus imagined that one day engineers would become practitioners of "climatological judo."

Taking part in the modern debates about climate change, he might say, as he did in 1953 in a speech delivered in Washington, DC, "Climate control pertains to all phases of the earth's water substance and temperature and winds (important principally as the carriers of water substance and heat). . . . If the present annual world rainfall were suitably described in space and time, there would be ample [rainfall] available."

He would likely ponder and then articulate the useful aspects of climatic shifts. He would challenge engineers, inventors, and entrepreneurs to engage in designing and building products to capitalize on the new temperature regimes and rainfall patterns. In the 1970s, still thinking about the bending of sound waves in water and what the bathythermograph revealed, Spilhaus proposed using sound waves to explore the temperature profiles of the ocean. Linking the profiles to satellite measurements of surface temperature, he believed scientists could calculate the bulk heat storage in a way that would be "a powerful input to the possible foreshadowing of climate."

One thing is for sure: he would not support any "zero risk" policy. "Zero risk will stifle inventiveness," he said to Louise O'Conner, echoing his sentiments in presentations and interviews since the mid 1970s.

"Zero risk." Nonsense! There must be more realistic awareness in all activities that there is an acceptable risk and that it is not zero.

"Zero effluents." Nonsense! There must be more awareness that in the use of the components of our environment—air, land and water—there is an acceptable burden of man's wastes of the proper kind that these components can carry and that this is not zero.

There must be awareness that water and air are commodities that we must use, clean and reuse, just as the commodity food is grown, used and re-grown. We must think of the culture of our air and water—atmoculture and hydroculture, if you like—as we think of agriculture today. We must realize that there is a cost for these new commodities, air and water. We must realize that cleaning up is not a one-shot proposition, but a continual added cost to the commodities that we borrow from our environment. Under-pricing water, air and energy promotes the waste of them, and thus, promotes pollution.

No, Dr. Spilhaus would not have been silent about climate. His grandest satisfaction came from stimulating people into action with exciting ideas. "It's more important to get out of the rut of our thinking," he said. "We must abandon traditional patterns. Being practical isn't the end-all and be-all of ideas."

At another time he explained, "I share the worries of people who think science is moving so fast that it may do terrible things, but I say 'All right, let's worry, but let's not stop science, let's make it a part of everything.'" He thought scientists were starting to spend too much time observing and not enough time solving problems. He said that resources need to be extracted and that you don't preserve the ecology by ruining the economy. His challenge to today's scientists and ecologists might be this: do something useful with all the data you are collecting.

At a 1972 lecture in Madison, Wisconsin, the revered Dr. Spilhaus advocated for innovation. "You are also working on the problem of so-called waste heat. During many months of the year in this frigid atmosphere, no heat could be waste heat! The challenge is how to use this heat in the year's few hot months." Dr. Spilhaus thought society's energy problems remain rooted in the fact that we've failed at emulating nature's ability to store energy. "Nature was able to store energy in the fossil fuels that were laid down over millions of years and which we use up in a very short time; but, we have not emulated nature in equivalent ways of storing energy."

Ever witty, Spilhaus said, "The residents of Cape Cod may not like to see their landscape spoiled by power and heating plants, but they still want heat and light. . . . You can't have your Cape and heat it too."

Athel and biographer Louise O'Connor spent many hours discussing the environment. At times, she said he seemed environmentally insensitive, but after years of conversations with him, she

Athelstan contemplating a version of his sun dial, circa 1990. Photo courtesy of the Dolph Briscoe Center for American History, University of Texas at Austin.

realized that he simply wholeheartedly believed in humankind's ability to simultaneously use and conserve resources. "Athel, as always, was practical in his approach to protecting the environment," said O'Connor. "He defended technology and science while at the same time recognizing and working to preserve our planet and its resources."

Spilhaus repeatedly said that what society calls waste "is some useful substance that we haven't the wit to use." For decades he devoted considerable time to what now might be termed "sustainability issues," but what he called "steadying the biological and physical state of the world." He reminded many lecture halls filled with people, "We are not consumers, but temporary users of materials." At a colloquium in April 1971, Athelstan gave a presentation, "Toward a Steady World," in which he spoke about our species' aspiration to survive. He said, "Everyone knows that in a world where the population, and along with it, raw materials and energy consumption grows at an exponential rate, the end result can only be disastrous."

"As an engineer and a doer," he said, "I reject the solution that says that people must do with less and go without in order to use lesser things. Yet the proper use of technology can, by striving for more energy economy and material thrift, give us all the services we need with the use of less of the materials that we're short of."

A striking feature of Athelstan Spilhaus's visions of the future is their relevance to contemporary concerns. In Todd Wildermuth's words, the perhaps overly optimistic Spilhaus believed that "science and technology were unquestionably good; the future would be better than the past; radical changes are preferable to gradual change; physical and chemical science dominated; and technocrats were sound judges of public welfare."

In the mid-1960s, before laptops and the Internet, Spilhaus was already speaking of the electronic delivery of news through a feedback system. In his mind, he saw a multichannel cable TV system that would allow a viewer to dial in and zoom to a particular item in the news. But using computers to assist in *printing* newspapers was the first idea Spilhaus pursued in synch with his newspaper publishing friends in Minneapolis and his tech-savvy associates. After that he considered the delivery of the news. It now seems that he possessed a crystal ball when he chaired the scientific advisory board of the American Newspaper Publishers Association. "When I talked about using pictures from satellites in the newspaper business back in the early 1960s, I was thought an absolute dreamer," he said.

Challenging the people attending the American Newspaper Publishers Association's annual convention in 1973, he said, "I asked publishers some time ago, 'What are you going to do when the printed page no longer is printed and is no longer on a page?' And I speculated with you then about the dial-a-newspaper, the synergism of newspapers and cable television techniques and the switching technologies of telephones."

When Spilhaus worked on his unpublished autobiography, *Spilly!*, with the assistance of Joe Brown in the 1970s, the phenomenon hadn't come to fruition. "It will," he wrote. And it did: in the form of personal computers, the Internet, and electronic publishing. And publishers are still in a quandary about what to do about it.

The University of Minnesota's Scholar's Walk in Minneapolis dedicates an area to Dr. Spilhaus. During an event commemorating the former dean's one hundredth birthday, Louise O'Connor stood by the rendition of the bathythermograph patent etched there and sighed, "I miss Athel every day." Despite the way the world has raced on since Athelstan Frederick Spilhaus passed away, his ideas continue to roil our imaginations and our world society.

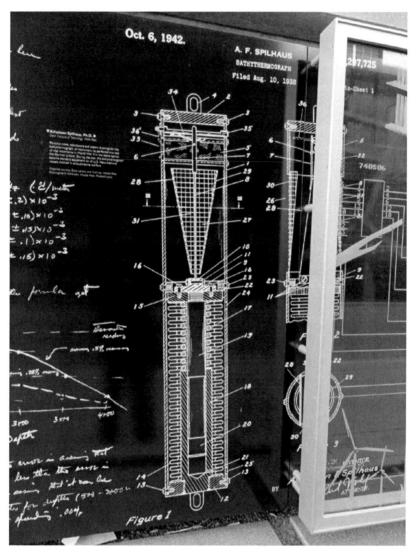

Bathythermograph diagram on the Wall of Discovery at the University of Minnesota Twin Cities. Photo by Sharon Moen.

For instance, the Utopia floating island structure now being developed by Yacht Island Design and BMT Nigel Gee seems like a direct Spilhaus descendant. Athelstan first floated the idea publicly in his *Our New Age* comic strip and later in a 1989 speech at the International Symposium on Coastal Ocean Space Utilization. There he proposed a project he wanted to call Project FORE (Floating Ocean Real Estate), then suggested with an ever-present twinkle in his eye that maybe, if the names weren't already taken, he would have called it Project FORD (Floating Ocean Realty Development) or TOYOTA (The Ocean You Ought to Occupy).

If it is possible to take away lessons from someone else's life, Spilhaus's showed that living up to one's intellectual potential can span decades, disciplines, continents—and that such lofty pursuits might require a high familial sacrifice. Spilhaus's ideals and ideas live through Sea Grant, within NOAA, and in myriad other ways such as skywalks, sculptures, economic planning, and pollution control. Spilly's was a trajectory of genius coupled with unflagging drive. His hearty appetite for joviality didn't diminish his demands for sharp thinking and productive activities. Dr. Spilhaus's life was remarkable, his energy enormous, his accomplishments inspiring, and his vision for the future hopeful.

The beautiful thing about science is not all the things
we know, but all the things we don't know.
To a scientist, the only things worth explaining
are the hitherto inexplicable. The only things
worth doing are the truly impossible.

—ATHELSTAN FREDERICK SPILHAUS

ATHELSTAN SPILHAUS'S CREDENTIALS

*The following record of Athelstan Spilhaus's credentials
is adapted from one found on Athelstan's desk
in Middleburg, Virginia, upon his death.*

Origins and Citizenship

Born Cape Town, Union of South Africa, November 25, 1911;
son of Karl Antonio and Nellie (Muir) Spilhaus; emigrated to
the United States, 1931; naturalized as U.S. citizen, 1946

Education

B. Sc., University of Cape Town, 1931

S.M., Massachusetts Institute of Technology, 1933

D. Sc., University of Cape Town, 1948

D. Sc. (Honorary), Coe College, 1961

D. Sc. (Honorary), Rhode Island University, 1968

D. Sc. (Honorary), Hahnemann Medical College, 1968

D. Sc. (Honorary), Philadelphia College of Pharmacy and Science, 1968

L. L. D. (Honorary), Nova University, 1970

D. Sc. (Honorary), Hamilton College, 1970

D. Sc. (Honorary), Southeastern Massachusetts University, 1970

D. Sc. (Honorary), Durham University, England, 1970

D. Sc. (Honorary), University of South Carolina 1971

D. Sc. (Honorary), Southwestern at Memphis, 1972

D. Sc. (Honorary), University of Maryland, 1978

Professional Career

Member, National Maritime Center Foundation, 1988–1998

President, Pan Geo, Inc., 1984–1998

Faculty Member, World Business Council, Casa de Campo, Dominican Republic, 1982

Visiting Fellow, Institute for Marine and Coastal Studies, University of Southern California, 1981–1983

Distinguished Scholar, Annenberg Center for the Study of the American Experience, University of Southern California, 1981

Consultant, National Oceanic and Atmospheric
Administration, 1980–1985

Member, Subcommittee, National Advisory Council on
Oceans and Atmosphere, 1980–1983

Distinguished Visiting Professor of Marine Sciences,
University of Texas, 1977–1978

Faculty Member, Young Presidents' Organization, Sydney,
Australia, 1977

Chairman, Advisory Committee to the Trustees, University
of Florida, 1976–1977

Phi Beta Kappa Visiting Scholar, fifteen universities, 1975–
1976

University Visiting Professor, Texas A & M University,
1974–1975

Special Assistant to the Administrator for Ocean and
Atmospheric Problems, National Oceanic and Atmospheric
Administration, 1974–1980

Fellow, Woodrow Wilson International Center for Scholars,
1971–1974

Chairman, American Association for the Advancement of
Science, 1971

President, American Association for the Advancement of
Science, 1970

Superintendent of Schools, Palm Beach County, Florida, 1970

President-Elect, American Association for the Advancement
of Science, 1969

President, Aqua International, Inc., 1969–1970

President, The Franklin Institute, Philadelphia, Pennsylvania, 1967–1969

Professor of Geophysics, University of Minnesota, 1966–1967

Dean, Institute of Technology, University of Minnesota, 1949–1966

Meteorological Adviser, Union of South Africa Government, 1947

Director of Research, New York University, 1946–1948

New York University, Meteorology Department: Assistant Professor, 1937; Department Chairman, 1938–1947; Associate Professor, 1939; Professor, 1942–1948

Woods Hole Oceanographic Institution: Research Assistant in Oceanography, 1936–1937; Investigator in Physical Oceanography, 1938–1960; Associate in Physical Oceanography, 1960; Honorary Staff Member, 1960–

Assistant Director of Technical Services, Union of South Africa Defense Forces, 1935–1936

Research Assistant, Massachusetts Institute of Technology, 1933–1935

Military and Related Service

U.S. Army Air Forces, 1943–1946

Scientific Director of Weapons Effects, two Nevada Atomic Tests, 1951

Consultant, Armed Forces Special Weapons Project,
Department of Defense, 1952

Member, Baker Mission to Korea, U.S. Army, 1952

Member and Chairman, Research and Development
Advisory Council, U.S. Army Signal Corps, 1950–1959

Member, Scientific Advisory Board, U.S. Air Force

Presidential Appointments

Envoy to the Union of South African Meteorological Service,
1947 (appointed by President Truman)

Executive Board of UNESCO, 1954–1958 (appointed twice
by President Eisenhower)

United States Commissioner, Seattle World's Fair, 1961–1963
(appointed by President Kennedy)

Member, National Science Board, 1966–1972 (appointed by
President Johnson)

Professional Society Memberships

Fellow, Royal Meteorological Society

Fellow, American Institute of Aeronautics and Astronautics

Fellow, American Association for the Advancement of Science

Member, Royal Society of South Africa

Fellow, American Geophysical Union

Fellow, World Academy of Art and Science

Member, American Meteorological Society

Member, American Society of Limnology and Oceanography

Member, American Philosophical Society

Industrial Affiliations

Member, Board of Trustees, Aerospace Corporation

Member, Board of Directors, Donaldson Company, Inc.

Member, Board of Directors, American Dynamics Corporation

Member, Board of Directors, Pergamon Press, Inc.

Member, Board of Directors, Franklin GNO

National Vice Chairman, Invest in America National Council, Inc.

Member, Board of Directors, Gould-National Batteries, Inc.

Consultant, General Electric Company, 1952–1954

Consultant, General Mills, 1950–1958

Consultant, Honeywell, Inc., 1954–1964

Inventions

Air condition indicator (Patent US2107017 issued February 1938)

Bathythermograph (Patent US2297725 issued October 1942)

Sea sampler (Patent US2314372 issued March 1943)

Calculator (Patent US2567246 issued September 1951)

Spilhaus space clock (Patent US3248866 issued May 1966)

Geared escapement device (Patent US3393909 issued July 1968)

Magnetic rolling device (Patent US3446999 issued May 1969)

Method of skating and apparatus (Patent US3442522 issued May 1969)

Descending music box (Patent US3535819 issued October 1970)

Beaded chain-descending toy (Patent issued US3590519 issued July 1971)

Tide computation apparatus and method (Patent US3745313 issued July 1973)

Map puzzle having periodic tessellated structure (Patent US4627622 issued December 1986)

Geographical sundial (Patent US4520572 issued June 1985)

Published Works

See the References for his books, comic strips, government reports, and more than 200 articles in scientific journals and magazines.

Honorary Societies

Sigma Xi

Tau Beta Pi

Awards and Honors

Legion of Merit Award, 1946

Exceptional Civilian Service Medal, United States Air Force, 1952

Patriotic Civilian Service Award, Department of the Army, 1959

Berzelius Medal, Sweden, 1962

Proctor Prize, Scientific Research Society of America, 1968

Fifteenth Anniversary Award, Marine Technology Society, 1977

Compass Distinguished Achievement Award, Marine Technology Society, 1981

First Spilhaus Symposium, "Arctic Ocean Engineering for the 21st Century," Marine Technology Society, October, 1984

Clubs

Cosmos Club, Washington, DC

The Explorers Club, New York

The Bohemian Club, San Francisco

Racquet Club, Philadelphia

Professional Affiliations

Member, Advisory Panel, Committee on Science and Astronautics, House of Representatives

Member, Board of Directors, Year of the Ocean Foundation

Chairman, Scientific Advisory Committee, American Newspaper Publishers Association

Member, Council on Trends and Perspective, Chamber of Commerce of the United States

Member, Editorial Board, Marine Technology Society Journal

Chairman, Committee on Pollution, National Academy of Sciences National Research Council (NAS-NRC)

Committee on Oceanography, NAS-NRC (Chairman, 1961–1964)

Board of Directors, American Association for the Advancement of Science

Board of Trustees, Science Service, Inc.

Executive Committee, Task Force on Resources, Recreation, and Conservation of the Commission on 1976, American Academy of Arts and Sciences

Advisory Board, World Book Encyclopedia Science Service

Chairman, American Editorial Board, The Commonwealth and International Library of Science, Technology, and Engineering

Honorary Editorial Advisory Board, Planetary and Space Physics

Editorial Advisory Board, *Industrial Research*

Editorial Advisory Board, *Oceanology*

Editorial Board, *The Underwater Yearbook*

Honorary Staff, Woods Hole Oceanographic Institution; Board of Trustees, 1950–1966

Board of Trustees, The International Oceanographic Foundation

Board of Trustees, Pacific Science Center Foundation

Board of Directors, American Museum of Archaeology

Board of Trustees, American Museum of Electricity

Board of Trustees; and Museum Committee, Saint Paul Institute

Board of Directors, North Star Research and Development Institute

Board, Louis W. Hill Award for the Outstanding Contribution to Space Transportation, Institute of Aerospace Sciences

Advisory Board, School of Environmental and Planetary Sciences, University of Miami

Advisory Board, Nova University

National Tuberculosis Association Commission on Air Conservation

Board of Directors, National Oceanography Association

Committee on Foreign Technical Cooperation, American Association of Land-Grant Colleges and State Universities

Governor's Committee of 100, State of Minnesota

Advisory Commission, State of Minnesota Department of Business Development

National Committee for the Florence Agreement

Governor's Oceanographic Advisory Council of Florida, 1964

Commissioner, Florida Commission on Marine Sciences and Technology, 1968

Study Committee on an Upper Midwest Research Institute

Committee Member, American Society for Engineering Education

Committee Member, Engineers' Council for Professional Development

Committee Member, National Society of Professional Engineers

Member, Panel on Development of Educational Motion Pictures and Lantern Slides in Meteorology, American Meteorological Society

Member, Public Information Conference, National Safety Council

Advisory Board, Space and Science Train, USA, Inc.

United States National Committee for the International Geophysical Year (IGY), NAS-NRC

USNC Technical Panel on the Earth Satellite, IGY

Committee on Polar Research, NAS-NRC

Geophysics Research Board, NAS-NRC

Committee on Natural Resources, NAS-NRC

Pacific Science Board, NAS-NRC

Special Study Group, National Academy of Sciences-Air Research and Development Command, 1957, 1958

Chairman, National Fisheries Center and Aquarium Advisory Board, United States Department of the Interior

Advisory Panel on Specialized Biological Facilities, National Science Foundation

United States National Commission, UNESCO

Advisory Panel on General Sciences, Office of the Secretary of Defense

Scientific Advisory Board, United States Air Force

Advisory Committee, Air Weather Service, United States Air Force

Research and Development Advisory Council, Army Signal Corps

Subcommittee on Meteorological Problems, National Advisory Committee for Aeronautics

Advisory Committee on Weather Services, Department of Commerce

Member, ad hoc Panel on Oceanography, Executive Office of the President, Office of Science and Technology

Engineering Advisory Committee, Associated University, Inc.

Member and Chairman, Standing Committee on Meteorology, Pacific Science Association

Chairman, Scientific Advisory Committee, Woods
Hole Oceanographic Institution; also, Member, Visiting
Committee of Department of Theoretical Oceanography
and Meteorology

Advisory Commission, Regional Committee on Marine
Sciences, Southern Regional Education Board

Visiting Committees on Meteorology, Aeronautical
Engineering, and Earth Sciences, Massachusetts Institute of
Technology

Committee on Education, American Geophysical Union

Committee on Extent of Air Space, International
Astronautical Federation

Comité Mondial, L'Université à l'Usine, Paris, France

Advisory Board, The Princeton Report

National Committee for the Florence Agreement

Governor's Oceanographic Advisory Council of Florida, 1964

Commissioner, Florida Commission on Marine Sciences and
Technology, 1968

Family

Maternal grandfather: Sir Thomas Muir, world-famous
mathematician

Paternal aunt: Nita Spilhaus, famous South African artist

Mother: Nellie Spilhaus, South African human rights
champion

Father: Karl Antonio Spilhaus, South African businessman

Brothers: Karl William (b. 1904), Thomas Muir (b. 1905)

Sisters: Margaret Virginia (b. 1908), Mary Antonia (b. 1909)

Wives: Mary Atkins, Gail Thompson (formerly Griffin), Kathleen Fitzgerald (formerly Clemente)

Children: A.F. Jr. (Fred), Mary Muir (Molly), Eleanor (Nellie), Margaret Ann, Karl

NOTES

Louise O'Connor documented recollections from Spilhaus, his siblings, his children, and his friends. Unless noted below, the quotations in *With Tomorrow in Mind* were collected by Ms. O'Connor and are archived at the Dolph Briscoe Center for American History, University of Texas at Austin.

Introduction: Spilly!

2   "I think the time has come: Ninety-Third Annual Meeting, 1964.

2   "When Athelstan Spilhaus had an idea: Wildermuth, 2008.

3   According to his FBI file: Federal Bureau of Investigation, 1966.

4   "Athel was a self-driven: Kathy Spilhaus, personal communication with Sharon Moen.

1. The Origins of a Force, 1911–1931

10   Carlos had been banished: Brown, circa 1975.

11   Diamond magnate Cecil Rhodes: Known for the De Beers diamonds, Rhodes's name also lived on in Rhodesia (the former name of Zimbabwe) and the Rhodes Scholarships.

13   I would include Nellie Spilhaus: Death of Dr. Nellie Spilhaus, 1972.

13   "I got a much better education at home: Ryan, 1987.

13   high schools were teaching the three Ts: Bring back the 3Rs dean
      urges, 1957.

14   classical boarding school education: Ryan, 1987.

15   a "sand yacht" out of an automobile frame: The Wanderer, circa 1927.

2. Love and War, 1932–1948

19   "We never saw who picked them up: Ryan, 1987.

20   A 1935 issue of *Popular Science*: Registers heat and humidity, 1935.

20   "It transformed something as ethereal: Wildermuth, 2008.

21   Draper coauthored one of his first manuscripts: Draper and
      Spilhaus, 1934.

22   "When Aunt Mary and Uncle Athel: Claire Gace, personal
      communication with Sharon Moen.

24   The first completed and recorded journey from Cape Town: Court
      Treatt, 1927.

25   More than fifty years later: O'Connor, 1990a.

26   Dr. Carl-Gustaf Arvid Rossby: Byers, 1960.

26   "a Hollywoodian flair for dramatic: Byers, 1960.

26   as many would call it, genius: Hutchinson, 1990.

27   he patented an improved gyroscope: Wildermuth, 2008.

27   He wanted to understand how wind: Weir, 2001.

28   The torpedo-shaped instrument: Weir, 2001.

29   "It rendered water more legible: Wildermuth, 2008.

29   some unknown variable in the water itself: Wildermuth, 2008.

30   "We were trying to convince them: Weir, 2001.

30   The BT enabled them: Wildermuth, 2008.

31   In [his earlier writings], Spilhaus described natural: Wildermuth,
      2008.

32   Winston Churchill wrote Spilhaus: Vadus, 1992.

33   The five-foot-eight, 180-pound major: Military files, Dolph Briscoe
      Center for American History, University of Texas at Austin.

37   In fact, the NYU Balloon Group: McAndrew, 1995.

3. Internationalist in the Heartland, 1949–1962

43   "Spilhaus was a great wanderer: Misa and Seidel, 2010.

44   "If becoming a dean: Wildermuth, 2008.

45   Perhaps the audience at the 1953: Wildermuth, 2008.

46   "Representation at UNESCO caused: Abel, 1998.

48   Originally, the lawnmower was just: O'Connor, 1990b.

49   "We watched you for two years: O'Connor, 1990b.

52   Now the moon shows: Flanagan, circa 1958.

52   "By exploding bombs: Flanagan, circa 1958.

56   tavern-owning newspaper columnist: The Wanderer, circa 1960.

57   "a chubby cheerful man of science: The Wanderer, circa 1960.

57   "I love to try something: Educator in orbit, 1959.

57   issued at least one DUI: University of Minnesota Archives.

59   President Lyndon Johnson gave out: Livezey, 1981.

59   "I don't do 'so many things: Cohn, 1962.

61   "Festival of the West: Rydell, et al., 2000.

62   Boeing donated the spacearium: U.S. Science Exhibit, 1963.

64   He got Michigan Island: Mrs. Spilhaus granted divorce, 1964.

64   he made life exciting: Claire Gace, personal communication with Sharon Moen.

64   Athel wed Gail Thompson Griffin: Dr. Athelstan Spilhaus will wed, 1964.

65   "As early as 1961: Wildermuth, 2008.

65   (If Spilhaus had his "cheeky way: Wildermuth, 2008.

4. MXC, 1962–1973

67   energy as the "fundamental currency: Spilhaus, 1973g, and elsewhere in articles and lectures.

68   "The younger Spilhaus: Wildermuth, 2008.

68   "During those critical years: Wildermuth, 2008.

69   "it had to be populated: Wildermuth, 2008.

70   "I dream of a city: O'Connor, 1990b.

71   "the screaming ambulances: Spilhaus, 1967b.

71   It struck him as ridiculous: Spilhaus, 1967b.

71   "these people are taken care of: Spilhaus, 1967b.

72   "I was on a HUD advisory committee: O'Connor, 1990b.

73   "one of the greatest minds that God: Wildermuth, 2008.

74   "the whole damn thing: O'Connor, 1990b.

74   "Bucky was a genius: O'Connor, 1990b.

74   "He ate an absolutely regular diet: O'Connor, 1990b.

75   "Without exception our cities: Cities under glass, 1968.

76   "the City was a seed: Wildermuth, 2008.

76   "I have great sympathy: Brown, circa 1975.

77   "sought to protect its newly acquired: Wildermuth, 2008.

77   "We obviously did not come prepared: Minnesota Experimental
       City Authority, 1963–1973.

78   city could create 130,000 new jobs: The newest new town, 1973.

78   slanderous editorials in early February: Wildermuth, 2008.

78   "get Spilhaus and his ideas: O'Connor, 1990b.

79   "The question of cities in the sea: O'Connor, 1990b.

79   "I'm impatient with the past: Cohn, 1962.

5. Sea Grant, 1963–Today

82   A few minutes later: Ninety-Third Annual Meeting, 1964.

84   "The excitement generated: Knauss, 1966.

85   "Like a military operation: Spilhaus, 1966a.

85   "ocean engineering problems are special: Sea Grant Colleges
       Hearings, 1966.

86   "The harvesting and husbandry of the food: Spilhaus, 1966a.

86   Dr. Spilhaus proposed using porpoises: Livezey, 1981.

87   "Basic funds, undesignated except: Spilhaus, 1964c.

87   "I wanted an EXACT parallel: Brown, circa 1975.

88   "Why do we know less: Spilhaus, 1973k, and elsewhere.

89   "One thing that struck me: Sea Grant Colleges Hearings, 1966.

90   The Congress finds and declares: National Sea Grant College
       Program Act, 1966.

90   "the most murderous and competent: Miloy, 1983.

91   "During the course of the program: Claiborne Pell, personal communication with Louise O'Connor.

91   "a tremendous ability to coin: John Knauss, personal communication with Louise O'Connor.

92   "the stewardship of resources: Spilhaus, 1976d.

93   "Inventing," he wrote later: Brown, circa 1975.

93   "I was interested in your studies: Spilhaus, 1973m.

94   "I think it's exceeded my expectations: Spilhaus, 1985b.

6. Momentum Toward Tomorrow, 1966–1978

95   "The colorful, quotable: U Dean Spilhaus will be "gadfly," 1966.

95   Wilson was publicly chiding Spilhaus: Anderson, 1967; Spilhaus: "U" has become great mediocrity, 1967.

96   a few newspaper clips: Clips are from 1967, of unknown origins, archived at the Anderson Library, University of Minnesota.

96   "It is hard to imagine a scientist: Undated newspaper article printed in Philadelphia, archived at the Dolph Briscoe Center for American History, University of Texas at Austin.

97   Anti-Spilhaus sentiments included: Newspaper article printed in Philadelphia, 1968, archived at the Dolph Briscoe Center for American History, University of Texas at Austin.

100   "he filed suit testing Florida's: Spilhaus quits congressional race, 1970.

100   "set off a flurry of political rumors: Spilhaus quits congressional race, 1970.

101   He made news headlines: Tryk, 1970.

105   "ecolibrium," his moniker: Spilhaus, 1972d.

106   "I'm trying to find out who is steering: Brown, 1974.

7. Leaving the World in Better Shape, 1979–1998

All quotes attributed to Kathy Spilhaus and thoughts about her life with Athel reflect conversations between the author and Ms. Spilhaus in 2010, with the following exceptions:

111   "For someone who has invented machinery: O'Connor, 1990b.

112   "A world map is a mathematical picture: Spilhaus, 1976b.

114   too narrow to constitute "real ocean: Braddock, 1989.

8. Work and Play Are Indistinguishable, 1911–1998

118   "the worst custody fight: Solis-Cohen, 1993.

119   "Old ones combine beauty: Solis-Cohen, 1993.

119   "engage in research, collection, renovation: Archived documents
       at the Dolph Briscoe Center for American History, University of
       Texas at Austin.

120   Ptak had driven down: Story of Ptak's visit with Spilhaus from John
       Ptak, personal communication with Sharon Moen.

123   "He was a role model: Joe Vadus, personal communication with
       Sharon Moen.

123   he probably died of heart failure: Kathy Spilhaus, personal
       communication with Sharon Moen.

124   poignant announcement: Woods Hole Oceanographic Institution,
       1998.

Epilogue

All comments from Spilhaus's friends are through Louise O'Connor's
correspondences archived at the Dolph Briscoe Center for American
History, University of Texas at Austin.

131   "I am not really much of a futurist: Livezey, 1981.

131   She said Athel worried: Kathy Spilhaus, personal communication
       with Sharon Moen.

131   "Athelstan was seldom without: Louise O'Connor, personal
       communication with Sharon Moen.

132   "The thermostat of the world: Spilhaus, 1964g.

132   "climatological judo: Wildermuth, 2008.

132   "Climate control pertains: Lewis et al., 1954.

132   "a powerful input: Spilhaus, 1976c.

133   "Zero risk." Nonsense! There must: Oral transcript with Louise
         O'Connor archived at the Dolph Briscoe Center for American
         History, University of Texas at Austin.

133   "You are also working: Spilhaus, 1973m.

134   "The residents of Cape Cod: Spilhaus, 1985a.

135   what he called "steadying: Spilhaus, 1972d.

135   "We are not consumers: Spilhaus, 1972d.

135   "Everyone knows that in a world: Spilhaus, 1971j.

135   "science and technology were unquestionably good: Wildermuth,
         2008.

136   "I asked publishers some time ago: Spilhaus, 1973n.

136   "It will," he wrote: Brown, circa 1975.

136   Athelstan first floated the idea: Spilhaus, 1990a.

REFERENCES

Works by Athelstan Spilhaus

An extensive (nearly exhaustive) list of publications by Athelstan Spilhaus.

1931.   The maintenance and operation of marine diesels. Journal of the
           University of Cape Town Engineering and Scientific Society 4(2):
           12-20.
1934a.   Analysis of the cup anemometer (with Carl Rossby).
           Massachusetts Institute of Technology Meteorological Course
           Professional Notes No. 7.
1934b.   The contribution of the gyroscope to safety in the air. Tech
           Engineering News 14: 154-155, February.
1934c.   Estimation of skill in forecasting. Bulletin of the American
           Meteorological Society 15: 281-282, December.
1934d.   Power supplies for suction-driven gyroscopic aircraft instruments
           (with C.S. Draper). Transactions of the American Society of
           Mechanical Engineers 56: 289-294, May.

1934e.   Speed of air driven rotors in gyroscopic instruments. Journal of the Institute of Aeronautical Sciences 1: 44-46, January.

1935a.   An air mass indicator. Bulletin of the American Meteorological Society 16: 31-33, February.

1935a.   The cup anemometer in an unsteady wind. Bulletin of the American Meteorological Society 16: 301-302, December.

1935b.   A new design of a dewpoint and temperature recorder. Bulletin of the American Meteorological Society 16: 119-122, May.

1935c.   The transient condition of the hair hygrometer. Bulletin of the American Meteorological Society 16: 217-218, October.

1935d.   The transient condition of the human hair hygrometric element. Massachusetts Institute of Technology Meteorological Course Professional Notes 8: 3-18.

1936a.   Diurnal changes in the free atmosphere over Pretoria. The South African Geographical Journal 19: 80-89, December.

1936b.   A study of the aspiration psychrometer. Transactions of the Royal Society of South Africa 24: 185-202.

1937a.   New method of nocturnal wind sounding. Bulletin of the American Meteorological Society 18: 154, April-May.

1937b.   Nocturnal wind sounding by photographic means (reply to Whipple's criticism in Meteorological Magazine, September). Meteorological Magazine 72: 229-230, November.

1937c.   Note the flow of streams in rotating systems. Sears Foundation Journal of Marine Research 1(1): 29-33, November.

1937d.   Results of aerological investigations in South Africa. Beitrage zur Physik der freien Atmosphare 24(3): 228-230.

1937–
1938.   A bathythermograph. Sears Foundation Journal of Marine Research 1: 95-100.

1938a.   Hyperbolic dividers for geostrophic wind computations. Bulletin of the American Meteorological Society 19: 351-353, October.

1938b.   Isentropic airplane flights—a suggestion. Bulletin of the American Meteorological Society 19: 279-280, September.

1938c.   Review of George F. Taylor: Aeronautical Meteorology. Journal of the Aeronautical Sciences 6(1): 32, November. Also in Bulletin of the American Meteorological Society 20: 62-63, February 1939.

1939a.   Development in meteorology (Part I of Recent Progress in
         Aeronautics). Mechanical Engineering 61: 150-151, February.

1939b.   On the transient of the ice bulb in psychrometric observations.
         Bulletin of the American Meteorological Society 20: 310-311,
         September.

1940a.   Comment on Refsdal's "Aerogram" and the "Tephigram."
         Bulletin of the American Meteorological Society 21: 1-3, January.

1940b.   A detailed study of the surface layers of the ocean in the
         neighborhood of the Gulf Stream with the aid of rapid measuring
         hydrographic instruments. Sears Foundation Journal of Marine
         Research 3(1): 51-75, May.

1940c.   Development in meteorology (Part VI of Recent Progress in
         Aeronautics). Mechanical Engineering 62: 115-116, February.

1940d.   Memorandum on suggested instrumental equipment for the
         study of wind temperature and humidity gradients in connection
         with questions of the interaction between the sea and the
         atmosphere (appendix to Report of Committee on Questions of
         Interaction between the Sea and the Atmosphere). Association
         d'Oceanographie Physique, Procès-Verbaux 3: 95-102.

1940e.   Rapid-measuring hydrographic instruments (abstract of a
         communication at the General Assembly of the International
         Association of Physical Oceanography, Washington, DC,
         September 1939). Association d'Oceanographie Physique, Procès-
         Verbaux 3: 192. Also: Committee Reports and Abstracts of
         Communications. Association d'Oceanographie Physique Union
         Geodesique et Geophysique Internationale General Assembly,
         Washington, DC, September 1939, 87.

1940f.   The shear stability ratio vector and its use in isentropic analysis.
         Bulletin of the American Meteorological Society 21: 239-248,
         June.

1941a.   Examples and outline of certain modifications in upper-air
         analysis (with R.B. Montgomery). Journal of the Aeronautical
         Sciences 8: 276-283, May.

1941b.   Fine structure of the edge of the Gulf Stream. Transactions of
         1941 of the American Geophysical Union, 478-484.

1941c.   Status of ozone measurements in New York City (with L. Carstansen and C. Hall). Transactions of the American Geophysical Union, 435-437.

1942a.   Maps of the whole world ocean. Geographical Review 32: 431-435, July.

1942b.   Review of H.U. Sverdrup, oceanography for meteorologists. Geographical Review 32(4).

1942c.   Workbook in Meteorology (with James E. Hiller). McGraw-Hill Book Company, New York.

1946a.   Recent developments in meteorological equipment. Bulletin of the American Meteorological Society 27: 399-409, September.

1946b.   Review of Herbert G. Dorsey, Jr., some meteorological aspects of the Greenland Ice Cap. Geographical Review 36(3).

1948a.   Controlled-altitude free balloons (with C.S. Schneider and C.B. Moore), Journal of Meteorology 5:130-137, August.

1948b.   Drop size, intensity and radar echo of rain. Journal of Meteorology 5: 161-164.

1948c.   Let robot work for you. American Magazine 146(6): 47, December.

1948d.   Raindrop size, shape, and falling speed. Journal of Meteorology 5: 108-110, June.

1948e.   Report on the Meteorological Services for the Union of South Africa Government. Also as Verslag oor Meteorologiese Diens. Gedruk in die Unie Von Suid-Afrika Deur Die Staatsdrukker. Union of South Africa Government Printer, Pretoria.

1948f.   The Sea Sampler (with Arthur R. Miller). Journal of Marine Research 7: 370-385.

1948g.   Technical Report No. I, Balloon Group, Constant Level Balloon Project (with C. S. Schneider and C. B. Moore). New York University, Research Division, College of Engineering, New York, April.

1949a.   Bathythermograph sea sampler. Association d'Oceanographie Physique, Procès-Verbaux 4: 146-147. Union Geodesique et Geophysique Internationale General Assembly at Oslo, August, 1948. Secretariat de l'Association, Geofysisk Institutt, Bergen.

1949b. The dean's page. Minnesota Technology 30(1), 30(3). Also in 1950: 30(4), 30(5), 30(6), 30(8), 31(2).

1949c. Important intangibles in cooperative research. Proceedings of the Annual Meeting 1949, 1-8. Engineering College Research Council of the American Society for Engineering Education, at Troy, New York, June 20–22, 1949, College of Engineering, State University of Iowa, Iowa City.

1949d. Relax . . . let the robot do it. Science Digest 25(3): 78-83, March.

1949e. The university, industry, and government as a research team. Proceedings of the Symposium on Engineering Research, University of Minnesota Engineering Experiment Station Bulletin 29: 5-9.

1950a. Constant level balloons. Procès-Verbaux des Séances de l'Association de Météorologie, Vol. 2: 169. Memoires et Discussions, Union Geodesique et Geophysique Internationale, Huitième Assemblée Generale, Oslo, Norvege, August 1948. Secretariat, Association Internationale de Météorologie, de l'UGGI, Institut Royal Météorlogique de Belgique, Uccle, Belgique, June.

1950b. Hydrostatic instability in the ocean. Transactions of the American Geophysical Union 31: 213-215, April.

1950c. Institute of Technology. Minnesota Voice of the Alumni 49(6): 149-150, February.

1950d. Introduction to panel on Arctic problems (summary of remarks). Panel on Arctic Problems, 1. Fall Meeting report, October 23–25, 1950, Industrial Research Institute, Inc., New York.

1950e. Oscillations in the stratosphere and high troposphere (with G. Emmons and B. Haurwitz). Bulletin of the American Meteorological Society 31: 135-138, April.

1950f. Progress in meteorological instrumentation, 1920–1950. Bulletin of the American Meteorological Society 31: 358-364, December.

1950g. Seven photographs of Maoris taken in New Zealand at the time of the Seventh Pacific Science Congress, February 2–22, 1949. Also used in Murphy, Grace E. Barstow. The Maoris were our hosts. Natural History 59(1): 8-14, January.

1951a.   Introduction to section meeting on meteorology. Proceedings
of the Alaskan Science Conference of the National Academy of
Sciences and the National Research Council, Washington, DC,
November 9–11, 1950. National Research Council Bulletin 122:
74-75, April.

1951b.   Summary of Resources for University Research. Committee
on Relations with Military Research Agencies (A.F. Spilhaus,
Chairman), Engineering College Research Council, American
Society for Engineering Education, Cambridge, Massachusetts,
June.

1951c.   University Research Potential. Committee on Relations
with Military Research Agencies (A.F. Spilhaus, Chairman),
Engineering College Research Council, American Society for
Engineering Education, State Engineering Experiment Station,
Georgia Institute of Technology, June.

1951d.   Weathercraft: How to Build Your Own Weather Station. Viking
Press, New York.

1951e.   World weather network. Compendium of Meteorology, American
Meteorological Society, 705-710.

1952a.   Controlled altitude balloons and vertical motion in the high
atmosphere (abstract and discussion). Proceedings of the Seventh
Pacific Science Congress of the Pacific Science Association, Vol.
3, 125-126. R.E. Owen, Government Printer, Wellington, New
Zealand.

1952b.   Description of bathythermograph with water sampling apparatus
(summary of discussion). Proceedings of the Seventh Pacific
Science Congress of the Pacific Science Association, Vol. 3, 224.
R.E. Owen, Government Printer, Wellington, New Zealand.

1952c.   Summary of resources for university research (with John I.
Mattill). Journal of Engineering Education 42: 270-279, January.

1953a.   Meteorological Instruments (with Middleton Knowles). University
of Toronto Press, Toronto.

1953b.   Technology's contribution to the economic future of the state.
Minnesota Engineer 4(5): 5-7.

1953c.   Weather is the Nation's Business. The report of the Department of Commerce Advisory Committee on Weather Services (with Joseph J. George, Chairman, et al.). Washington, DC, United States Government Printing Office, December. Also in Extracts in Bulletin of American Meteorological Society 35(1), January 1954.

1954a.   Report of the delegates of the American Geophysical Union to the Fourth National Conference for UNESCO in Minneapolis, September 15–17, 1953 (with Donald B. Lawrence). Transactions of the American Geophysical Union 35: 188-189.

1954b.   Sea and air resources. Geographical Review 44: 346-351. Also in Oceanus 3(2): 5-11, Winter 1955.

1954c.   The way ahead for research in sea and air resources, in: The Nation Looks at Its Resources, 316-319. Resources for the Future, Inc., Washington, DC.

1955–   The oceans. The Quarterly of the American Interprofessional
1956.   Institute 30(2): 3-10, Winter.

1956a.   Control of our world environment: Its effect on land, sea and air resources. In Proceedings of the Twentieth Executives' Conference, May 10–11, 1956, 57-70. The Institute of Paper Chemistry, Appleton, WI.

1956b.   Control of the world environment. Geographical Review 46: 451-459.

1956c.   The International Geophysical Year, Progress Thru Research 10(4): 1-3, 11-13. Also Journal Madras University B 27(1): 211-223, 1957.

1956d.   Report of the Standing Committee on Meteorology of the Pacific. Proceedings of the Eighth Pacific Science Congress of the Pacific Science Association, 1953, Volume IIA, 918-926. National Research Council of the Philippines, Queson City.

1957a.   Aspects of the Atomic Energy Commission. In Problems of Journalism—1957, 214-219. American Society of Newspaper Editors, Wilmington, DE.

1957b.   Heavenly view of the heavens. Research and Engineering 3(6): 14-17.

1957c.   Science in Creative Living. Science Bulletin No. 5. Science Museum, Saint Paul Institute, St. Paul, MN.

1958–
1973.   Our New Age. An illustrated weekly (Sunday) feature on science published in newspapers in the United States and foreign countries. With Earl Cros from September 21, 1958, to April 1961; with Eugene Felton from May 1961 to October 1962; with Gene Fawcette from October 1962 to 1973.

1958a.   Earth, sun and space. Engineering Journal 10(6): 111-118. Also Proceedings of the Ninth Pacific Science Congress 1957 1: 78-82, 1958.

1958b.   How vehicles extend our reach in geophysics. Proceedings of the 38th Annual Meeting, American Petroleum Institute, 14-17.

1958c.   Implications of satellite development. In: National Security in the Nuclear Age, Center for International Relations and Area Studies, University of Minnesota Twin Cities, pp. 18-21.

1958d.   The purposes of schools. Shattuck Alumni Magazine 8: 67-70, Summer.

1958e.   Satellite of the Sun. Viking Press, New York. Also 1960, Arco Publications, London; 1961, Sansoni, Satellite del Sole in Florence, Italy; reprinted 1964, Atheneum Edition, New York.

1959a.   Assume a capability for manned space operations: For what purposes should this capability be utilized?, in: Alperin, M., Gregory, H.F. (Eds.), Vistas in Astronautics, Pergamon Press, New York, Vol. 2, pp. 142-144.

1959b.   Oceanography 1960 to 1970: A report by the Committee on Oceanography, National Academy of Sciences' National Research Council (with Harrison Brown, Chairman, et al.). National Academy of Sciences, Washington, DC.

1959c.   Research and the curriculum in colleges and universities: The sciences. The North Central Association Quarterly 33: 228-230, January.

1959d.   Turn to the Sea. National Academy of Sciences, Washington, DC.

1960a.   The panel discussion (with Dean Acheson, Frank D. Ashburn, John H. Finley, Jr., and Hrs. Reinhold Niebuhr). Quarterly (Seventy-fifth Anniversary Supplement), 1-18.

1960b.   Principal address at cornerstone laying ceremonies. General Mills Research Center, Progress Thru Research 14(1): 7, May.

1960c. Turn to the sea. UNESCO Courier Nos. 7-8: 5-17, July-August.

1961a. All land is an island. Navy 4: 33-35, July.

1961b. Turn to the Sea. Good Reading Rack Service Division, Koster-Dana Corporation, New York.

1962a. The dean's page. Minnesota Technolog 43(1): 7, October.

1962b. Man and the sea, in: McGraw-Hill Yearbook of Science and Technology, McGraw-Hill, Charlottesville, VA, pp. 41-52. Also in Natural Resources, National Academy of Sciences National Research Council, 1968.

1962c. Supplemental Appropriation Bill. Hearings 87th Congress, 1-16.

1962d. Turn to the Sea. Whitman Publishing Company, Racine, WI.

1962e. The United States Science Exhibit at the Seattle World's Fair. Weatherwise 15: 47-49, April.

1962f. The wonderful world of science. Minnesota Technolog 42(6): 8-9, 26-27.

1962g. The world of science. A and B Science News 9(1): 1,3, Fall.

1963a. Exploitation of the sea, in: Leydet, F. (Ed.), Tomorrow's Wilderness, Sierra Club, San Francisco, pp. 107-115.

1963b. Let robot work for you, in: Bailey, M., Leavell, U. (Eds.), A World to Discover, American Book Company, New York, pp. 602-608.

1963c. Math Teaching. Minimath Reports, University of Minnesota, Spring.

1963d. Oceanography's future. U.S. Naval Institute Proceedings 89: 24-37, November. Also in: Long, E.J. (Ed.), Ocean Sciences, U.S. Naval Institute, Annapolis, 1964.

1963e. U.S. Science Exhibit, Seattle World's Fair, Final Report. U.S. Government Printing Office, Washington, DC.

1964a. Engineering the oceans. Undersea Technology 5(5): 30-31.

1964b. Lots of Time. Edmund Scientific Company.

1964c. Man in the sea. Congressional Record, Appendix A3374-3375, June. Also in Science 145(3636): 393.

1964d. Marine technology and engineering the oceans, in: Buoy Technology: An Aspect of Observational Data Acquisition in Oceanography and Meteorology (supplement), Marine Technology Society, Washington, DC, pp. 1-4.

1964e.   Minneapolis Tribune Series: Earth: An ocean world, October
         26; Ocean reacts with atmosphere to provide world a thermostat,
         November 2; How, and why, do we ask questions of the ocean?
         November 9; New job for man: Ocean engineering, November 16.

1964f.   Oceanography: A wet and wondrous journey. Bulletin of the
         Atomic Scientists 20(10): 11-15, December.

1964g.   Technology, the engineer and the ocean, in: California and the
         World Ocean (conference proceedings), California Museum of
         Science and Industry, Los Angeles, pp. 43-45.

1965a.   The concept of a sea-grant university (speech delivered at the
         National Conference on Sea-Grant Colleges, Newport, Rhode
         Island, October 28, 1965); Congressional Record-Appendix,
         A6629-A6632, November 15. Also Proceedings of the Conference
         on the Concept of a Sea-Grant University, University of Rhode
         Island, Kingston, 5-12, 1966; reprinted, Vital Speeches of the Day
         XXXII(7): 212-216, 1966; Free Library of Philadelphia 815(83),
         V.32, 1965/66.

1965b.   Concepts of sea grant university, ocean engineering set forth.
         News Report, National Academy of Sciences' National Research
         Council, National Academy of Engineering 15(10): 4-5,
         December.

1965c.   The future of oceanography, in: Annual Report of the Board of
         Regents of the Smithsonian Institution, 1964, U.S. Government
         Printing Office, Washington, DC, pp. 361-371.

1965d.   A look at the problems of pollution. Minneapolis Tribune.
         September 26.

1965e.   New horizons in water engineering. Industrial Water Engineering
         2(8): 16-19, August.

1965f.   Remarks by Dr. Athelstan F. Spilhaus, Chairman of American
         Newspaper Publishers Association Scientific Advisory Committee.
         American Newspaper Publishers Association Convention Bulletin
         3: 24-30, April.

1966a.   The concept of a sea-grant university and Statement by Dr.
         Athelstan Spilhaus, Dean of the Institute of Technology,
         University of Minnesota, in: Hearings Before the Special

Subcommittee on Sea Grant Colleges of the Committee on Labor and Public Welfare, United States Senate, Eighty-Ninth Congress, Second Session, on S. 2439, May 2–5, 1966, U.S. Government Printing Office, Washington, DC, pp. 31-38, 196-201.

1966b. Exploiting the sea. Industrial Research 8(3): 62-68.

1966c. Goals in geotechnology. Transactions of the American Geophysical Union 47(2): 363-368, June. Also Bulletin of the American Meteorological Society 47(5): 358-363, May 1966.

1966d. Needed: The systems point of view. Air Force and Space Digest 49(10): 63-66, October.

1966e. Ocean engineering. Experimental Mechanics 6(7): 3A, July.

1966f. Preface, in: Careers in High-School Physics Teaching, American Institute of Physics, New York, May 1962.

1966g. Resourceful waste management. Science News 89(25): 486-488, June.

1966h. Waste Management and Control, A Report by the Committee on Pollution, National Academy of Sciences' National Research Council (Athelstan Spilhaus, Chairman, et al.), Washington, DC.

1967a. Experimental cities. The Next Ninety Years, Proceedings of a conference held at the California Institute of Technology March 1967, 149-169, California Institute of Technology, Pasadena.

1967b. The Experimental City. Daedalus: Journal of the American Academy of Arts and Sciences, Fall, 1129-1141. Also:

- reprinted in DE B.A.B. BOUWT, B.A.B. DEN HAAG (Holland) 50: 24-33
- reprinted as Cities to live in: The experimental city. Current Magazine, 40-49, January 1968
- edited version in Science Magazine, 710-715, February 1968
- reused in psychology workbook by Burgess Publishing Company, Minneapolis, 1968
- abstracted in EKISTICSS Magazine (Athens, Greece) 25(148): 135-138, March 1968
- edited version in Rotarian Magazine, March 1968
- reprinted in NICHIBEI FORUM (Japan-America Forum), 44-57, U.S. Information Service, Overseas Offices, May 1968

- translated and published in Das Ende der Stadte?, 51-65, Stuttgart, West Germany, 1968
- reprinted as part of the syllabus for Ideas and Living Today at Stephens College, Columbia, MO, 1968–1969
- combined version of article and address given December 27, 1967, at New York meeting of AAAS
- reprinted in DIALOGUE 2(1), U.S. Information Agency, 1969

1967c. The experimental city (a series of five articles). Minneapolis Tribune. January 23–27.

1967d. The Experimental City, UTOPIA. Charlatan Publishers, St. Cloud, MN.

1967e. Geotechnology objectives demand imaginative planning. Technology Week 20(4): 68-71, January.

1967f. No slums, no waste, no unemployment. Edison Electric Institute Bulletin, October.

1967g. The oceanic idea and the Sea Grant College. Navy 10(4): 48-53, April.

1967h. The Ocean Laboratory. Creative Educational Society, Inc., Mankato, MN, in cooperation with the American Museum of Natural History, New York.

1967i. Oceanography 1966: Achievements and Opportunities. A report of the Committee on Oceanography (Publication 1492), National Academy of Sciences' National Research Council (with Milner Schaefer, Chairman, et al.), Washington, DC.

1967j. Research needs in environmental health (remarks by Dean Spilhaus), in: A Symposium of the National Research Council held March 15, 1966, National Academy of Sciences (Publication 1419), Washington, DC, pp. 8-11.

1967k. The Scientific Advisory Committee. R.I. Bulletin 920: 136-137, May 29.

1967l. Sea in the service of man. Presentation archived at the Dolph Briscoe Center for American History, University of Texas at Austin.

1967m. Some new adventures in science. Franklin Institute. November.

1967n. Waste management and control. Scientist and Citizen, pp. 219-223, November–December.

1967o.   Waste management and control: Introduction and excerpts. Scientist and Citizen 9(1): 10-11, January.

1968a.   Are new cities the answer? Appalachia 1(8): 12-13, April.

1968b.   City of the Future—Experimental City. The American Museum of Natural History's Nature and Science—Teacher's Edition 5(14): 7-9, April.

1968c.   Daring experiments for living. Science Service, Washington, DC, March 4. Also in Congressional Record, March 6, 1968.

1968d.   The Experimental City. UNESCO Features 532(1): 9-13. Also in Science, February 16; and in: Pozweue, Sandler (Eds.), The Restless Americans: The Challenge of Change in American History, Volume 1, Xerox College Publishing, 1972.

1968e.   The Experimental City: A radical approach to housing problems. Technical Journal 98: 30-31.

1968f.   Man turns seaward. Today's Education 57(8), November.

1968g.   Population (Trends and Problems). Chemical and Engineering News, 102-104, October 14.

1968h.   De Proefstad. Intermediair, Netherlands.

1968i.   The role of technology in urban development. The Conference Board Record 5(11): 40-46, November.

1968j.   Sonic boom report. Science and Citizen 10(9), November.

1968k.   Synergism of doctor and engineer, Philadelphia Medicine 64(16): 725, 727, 729, 730, 731, August 20. Also in Hahnemann Alumni News, 13-16, Summer.

1968l.   Underwater Laboratory Symposium Proceedings. Keynote Address, September.

1969a.   Forum Interview. PILOT 23: 4-5, February.

1969b.   If trees could vote. Journal of Forestry, 8-10, January.

1969c.   Science and future. BAAS-AAAS Conference Summary, April.

1969d.   So that man might live better. Bell Telephone Magazine, 20-25, September/October.

1969e.   Technology, living cities and human environment. American Scientist 57(1): 24-36.

1969f.   Why have cities? The Science Teacher 36(9): 16-18, December.

1970a.   America's changing environment. The DAEDALUS Library, Volume 15, 219-231. Houghton Mifflin, Boston.

1970b.   A bold new concept of education. TWA Ambassador, 15, 16, May–June. Also Witchita Eagle, May.

1970c.   Comments from Panel on Science and Technology. 11th Meeting—Committee on Science and Astronautics, U.S. House of Representatives, 103-105, January.

1970d.   Confrontation with environment. 24th Annual Farm Forum Publication, March.

1970e.   An essay by Athelstan Spilhaus, in: Falk, I.A. (Ed.), Prophecy for the Year 2000, Julian Messner Pub, pp. 227-231.

1970f.   Leadership for tomorrow. Conference Participation—National Industrial Conference Board (by Holly McNamee) 7(1): 48-56, January.

1970g.   Letter from the president. American Association for the Advancement of Science Bulletin, September.

1970h.   Letter to AAAS Society, American Astronautical Society Newsletter 9(3): 2-3, July.

1970i.   Mobilizing to use the seas. The Report of the President's Task Force on Oceanography, June.

1970j.   Newspaper of the future. Newsprint Facts 14(3), May-June.

1970k.   The next industrial revolution. The Conference Board Record 7(2): 38-40, February. Also Science 167: 1673, March; Architects and Engineers Forum, Cities 1970, April; Proceedings of the Proprietary Association, 89th Meeting, 58-68, May; Reader's Digest, 169-170, July.

1970l.   Science yells for industry's help against pollution. Business Week, 62-63, January.

1970m. Two views of the environmental ecological problems. Environmental Design West 1(4): 14, August-September.

1971a.   The bathythermograph: An appreciation of Columbus Iselin. Oceanus XVI(2): 40, June.

1971b.   Dimensions of the environmental crisis, in: The Experimental City, Wiley, New York, pp. 187-205.

1971c.   Editorial, AAAS Meeting in Mexico City. Science, November.

1971d. Man's Return to the Sea. Sea Grant Publication No. TAMU-
SG-71-301, Texas A & M University, College Station, December.

1971e. Neuvas Ciudades. Carta Semanal, September 11 and 18.

1971f. The next industrial revolution. Letter No. 1, Bank of Commerce,
Toronto.

1971g. The Next Industrial Revolution. New Englander, 14-15, 18-19,
24-27, August. Also Proceedings of the American Philosophical
Society 115(4), August; Notiziario CTIP 13, January 1972.

1971h. A plan for living. Panhandle Magazine, 13-17, Summer.

1971i. La Prossima Rivoluzione Industriale. Operare 27: 30-37, August.

1971j. Toward a steady world. Colloquium presentation. April. Archived
at the Dolph Briscoe Center of American History, University of
Texas at Austin.

1971k. Waste management and control, in: Our World in Peril: An
Environment Review, Fawcett Premier Original, Greenwich, CT,
pp. 427-434.

1971l. Welcome to our members—Thanks to Philadelphia. AAAS
program, December.

1972a. Bountiful grants of the sea. First Annual Sea Grant Lecture,
MIT Sea Grant Program, MIT Report No. MITSG 73-1, Index
No. 73-90l-Weo. September. Also in Vital Speeches of the Day
XXXIX(12): 365-369, April 1973; Congressional Record, 119(71):
E-3124, May 1973. Reprinted as Engineering, ecology, and use of
the sea. National Fisherman, Yearbook issue, 1973.

1972b. City in the sea. Petroleum Today, December.

1972c. Coping with environmental problems, in: A Look at Business
in 1990, A Summary of the White House Conference on the
Industrial World Ahead, U.S. Government Printing Office,
Washington, DC, November, pp. 177-178.

1972d. Ecolibrium. Science 175:711-715, February 18. Also Virginia
Dental Journal 49(3): 26-36, June; Southwestern News 35(3): 3-4,
9, June; Ekistics 34(200): 4-5, July.

1972e. Ecolibrium, A Synopsis. Technolog, 17, May.

1972f. Land is just an island: Birth of the Sea Grant. EOS 53(5): 572-578,
May.

1972g.   MXC, a city with a taste of tomorrow, Assignment: Find a Better Way to Live. Special issue of Northwestern Bell Magazine, 37-42.

1972h.   Report to the Association, 1971. Science 175.

1972i.   Technology and resources for business. Wall Street Transcript, March.

1972j.   There is an acceptable burden of man's wastes. World Ecology 2000 3(20), October.

1973a.   Bountiful grants from the sea. The Saturday Evening Post, September/October.

1973b.   "Cities in the sea" could help solve environmental problems. The Battery Man, The International Journal for Starting, Lighting, Ignition and Generating Systems 15(3), March.

1973c.   Could "cities in sea" solve environment problems? Idaho Statesman. April.

1973d.   The creative community. Arts and Science Programs for New and Renewing Communities, Second Draft, February.

1973e.   Ecolibrium. Northwest Architect, 85-86, September-October.

1973f.   Ecolibrium—Or the New Industrial Revolution. Reclamation Industries International, Croydon, England, 27-33, September/ October.

1973g.   Energy: The fundamental currency of civilization. Annual Report of Dain, Kalman and Quail, Inc. Also Japan House Newsletter, February 1974.

1973h.   Engineering afloat: Toward a sea city. Technolog Review 75(3), January.

1973i.   Harmony of Man's Industry and Living Space. Claremont College, Claremont, CA.

1973j.   Inventing new cities. Harper's Magazine 246(1474): 8-9, March.

1973k.   The Oceans and National Economic Development. Proceedings of a Senate Commerce Committee Document (keynote address given at NOAA Conference, July 17, 1973, Seattle, Washington), December.

1973l.   The Oceans: Our Nation's Business. Center for Marine Resources and Sea Grant Program, Texas A & M University, College Station, November. Also Shell Oil's Ecolibrium (Elden Libby) 2(4), 1973.

1973m.   Sea Grant's challenge for the '70's, in: University of Wisconsin
         Annual Report, Sea Grant College, 1971–1972, pp. 20-21.

1973n.   The utmost is never enough, address given at the ANPA Labor
         Conference, Monday, April 23, 1973, Hotel Waldorf-Astoria, New
         York. American Newspaper Publishers Association Convention
         Bulletin 6, June.

1974a.   Changing patterns of science, in: International Symposium III,
         Battelle Memorial Institute, October, pp. 26-30.

1974b.   Pressures of the Mid-70's, in: American Newspaper Publishers
         Association Research Institute, pp. 153-156.

1975a.   Commercial ocean development. Marine Technology Society
         Journal 9: 40, September.

1975b.   Destinations: The newspaper odyssey. Production Conference
         Seminar, ANPA Research Institute, Bulletin 1197: 197-204,
         August.

1975c.   Ecolibrium, a balance between economy and ecology.
         Proceedings of First Annual Conference, The Coastal Society, 81,
         November.

1975d.   Geo-art: Plate tectonics and platonic solids. EOS 56(2), American
         Geophysical Union, February.

1975e.   Imagination: Key to invention and enterprise. Texas Business
         Executive, 3-19, Spring. Also Design Graphics Journal, Spring.

1975f.   A look into the future. Atlanta Historical Bulletin XIX(4): 77-90.

1975g.   National Science Foundation 1950–1975. EOS 56(9): 579,
         September.

1975h.   Population and energy balance. Theme Abstract: The
         Productivity Resources Environment Interface, 27, 28, June.

1975i.   A report of the conference on seaward advancement of industrial
         societies. Marine Technology Society Journal, 6-11, March.

1975j.   The sea I would like to see. The Rotarian, 28, 29, May. Also as El
         Mar que me Gustaria Ver, Revista Rotaria, 6-11, May.

1975k.   Striking a balance. Agricultural Engineering, 14-17, September.

1976a.   Evolution and description of a new sun sculpture. Disclosure
         document available at the Dolph Briscoe Center for American
         History, University of Texas at Austin.

1976b.   New look in maps brings out patterns of plate tectonics. Smithsonian Magazine, 54-63, August.

1976c.   Ocean stewardship with a view to productivity. Marine Technology Society Journal 10(7): 3-6.

1976d.   Speech at the celebration of the tenth anniversary of Sea Grant. Transcript available at the Dolph Briscoe Center for American History, University of Texas at Austin.

1977a.   Living without learning vs. learning without living: response to Clifford Simak's remarks. University of Minnesota Update 5(2).

1977b.   Mao Tse Tung. Piedmont Virginian, January.

1979.   To see the oceans, slice up the land. Smithsonian Magazine, 116-122, November.

1980.   A collector finds toys are not meant only for children. Smithsonian Magazine, 157-163, December.

1981a.   Be the first to sail straight around the world—almost! Virginia Country Magazine, 48-49, Winter.

1981b.   A new way of looking at the world (Whole World Ocean Map illustration), Calypso Log, 12, September.

1981c.   Toy country. Virginia Country Magazine, 42-47, Winter.

1981d.   The Yankee Mariner: Past, present and future. Sea Technology Magazine, 61, July.

1982a.   Map of the whole world ocean. Mapline, Harmon Dunlap Smith Center for the History of Cartography at the Newberry Library, No. 27, September.

1982b.   Miniature mechanical marvels. Technology Review 85(1), January.

1982c.   Sea power and the dilemmas of mankind, in: The Yankee Mariner and Sea Power, Center for the Study of the American Experience, The Annenberg School of Communications, University of Southern California Press, pp. 17-28.

1982d.   Spilhaus whole ocean maps I & II. Musical Six-Six Newsletter 11(2).

1983a.   An equal area map of the world with edges formed by major tectonic plate boundaries (an illustration). EOS 64(14), Transactions of the American Geophysical Union, April.

1983b. Oceans and reestablishing independence. Proceedings Oceans '83 Effective Use of the Sea, An Update, Marine Technology Society, 1167-1172, August/September.

1983c. World ocean maps: The proper places to interrupt. Proceedings of the American Philosophical Society 127(1): 50-60.

1984a. Engineering the Arctic Ocean—A National Challenge. Sea Technology Magazine, 73, September.

1984b. Plate tectonics in geoforms and jigsaws. Proceedings of the American Philosophical Society 128(3): 257-269.

1984c. Reestablishing our independence. Center for Marine Studies, Old Dominion University, Norfolk, VA, 2-15, January.

1984d. Sea power, past present and future. Center for Marine Studies, Old Dominion University, Norfolk, VA, 16-22, January.

1984e. Those wonderful old mechanical toys!, in: Encyclopedia Britannica, Yearbook of Science and the Future, pp. 24-45.

1985a. The challenge ahead: arctic science and engineering. Arctic Ocean Engineering for the 21st Century, Proceedings of the First Spilhaus Symposium, Marine Technology Society, 9-12.

1985b. The concept of a Sea Grant University. Sea Grant: Past, Present and Future, Sea Grant Association and University of Rhode Island, 19-28, October.

1985c. Energy and the oceans, a legal perspective. Keynote Address (April 3, 1982), Proceedings of the First Environmental Law Symposium. Journal of Law and the Environment, 57-64.

1985d. Forgotten inventors. Antique Toy World 15(1): 8-11, January.

1985e. The Puzzle of the Plates (a jigsaw puzzle and instruction manual). American Geophysical Union.

1985f. A series of educational games (The Spilhaus Geoglyph, GeOdyssey: The World Game, GeOdyssey Delux, GeoCards, Tectonicube, Flight Lines), Geolearning Corp., Sheridan, Wyoming.

1985g. World Ocean Map (poster), Geolearning Corp., Sheridan, Wyoming.

1986a. Hail to Halley's! (with Kathleen Fitzgerald Spilhaus). Virginia Country Magazine, 20-26. April.

1986b.   Martin: Marvelous mechanical manikins, the first epoch (with
         Kathleen Fitzgerald Spilhaus). Collectors' Showcase, 5-9.
         January–February.

1986c.   Martin: Marvelous mechanical manikins, the second epoch (with
         Kathleen Fitzgerald Spilhaus). Collectors' Showcase, 37-44. May–
         June.

1986d.   Our future oceans: Visions of a pragmatic idealist. Proceedings
         from the Annual Ocean Day Symposium, August 9, 1986, 37-48,
         Ocean Church, HSA Publications.

1987a.   Martin: Marvelous mechanical manikins, Part III: Continuations,
         copies and confusions (with Kathleen Fitzgerald Spilhaus),
         Collectors' Showcase, 51-55. March-April.

1987b.   On reaching 50: An early history of the bathythermograph. Sea
         Technology, 19-28, November.

1987c.   The stewardship of North America's great inland seas. Remarks
         at the dedication of NOAA's Great Lakes Environmental
         Research Laboratory, Ann Arbor, Michigan, April 27, 1987,
         available through the Dolph Briscoe Center for American History,
         University of Texas at Austin.

1988a.   Celebrating 25 years of ocean involvement, recollections: Dr.
         Athelstan Spilhaus. Sea Technology, 17-18, June.

1988b.   Our faith in the sea. Keynote Address, Annual Ocean Day
         Symposium, 1987, Ocean Perspectives Journal, Spring.

1989a.   Grandfather's Tool Town. Pan Geo, Inc., Middleburg, VA.
         Limited edition of 100. December.

1989b.   Mechanical Toys: How Old Toys Work (with Kathleen Spilhaus),
         Crown Publishers, New York. Also Robert Hale Ltd., London.

1989c.   The water planet map. Dolphin Log, 6-7, March.

1990a.   Artificial ocean islands, in: Halsey, S.D., Abel, R.B. (Eds.),
         Coastal Ocean Space Utilization, Proceedings of the First
         International Symposium on Coastal Ocean Space Utilization
         (COSU '89), Elsevier, New York.

1990b.   Epilogue: The unity of the ocean, in: Singer, S.F. (Ed.), The
         Ocean in Human Affairs, Paragon House, New York, pp. 355-
         358.

1990c. How we wrote our toy book (with Kathleen Spilhaus). Inside
        Collector, 75-77, July/August.

1991a. Atlas of the world with geophysical boundaries showing oceans,
        continents and tectonic plates in their entirety. Memoirs of the
        American Philosophical Society, Volume 196, May.

1991b. Colonization of the ocean. Sea Technology, 65-67, January.

1991c. World maps with natural boundaries (with John Snyder).
        Cartography and Geographic Information Systems 18(4): 246-
        254.

1993.   New equal area world map projections to better display polar
        regions. Proceedings of the American Philosophical Society
        137(2): 179-193, June.

1994.   Escheresch. The Lighter Side of Mathematics, Proceedings
        of the Eugene Strens Memorial Conference on Recreational
        Mathematics and Its History, Mathematical Association of
        America, 101-104.

1996.   World Map centered on Buenos Aires. International Symposium
        on Coastal Ocean Space (COSU '96), Preprints, December.

Other Sources

Abel, Robert, 1998. Eulogy for Dr. Athelstan Frederick Spilhaus.
    Minnesota Sea Grant archives.

Anderson, Mike, 1967. Wilson ashamed of Spilhaus; calls his remarks
    'nonsense.' Minnesota Daily. September 26.

Athelstan Frederick Spilhaus, inventor of aliens, died on March 30th, aged
    86. 1998. The Economist. April 9.

Athelstan's world. 1963. Newsweek. February 18, 1963.

Braddock, H.L., 1989. The water planet map. Dolphin Log, The Cousteau
    Society, 6-7, March.

Briggs, P., 1968. Men in the Sea. Simon and Schuster, New York.

Bring back the 3Rs dean urges. 1957. Austin Daily Herald. December 24.

Brown, Joseph, 1974. The visions of a pragmatic idealist. Exxon USA, no.
    4 (4th Quarter): 10-12.

Brown, Joseph, circa 1975. Spilly! Unpublished autobiography crafted in cooperation with Athelstan Spilhaus. Available through the Dolph Briscoe Center for American History, University of Texas at Austin.

Byers, Horace, 1960. Carl-Gustaf Arvid Rossby 1898–1957: Biographical Memoir. National Academy of Sciences, Washington, DC. www .nasonline.org/publications/biographical-memoirs/memoir-pdfs/ rossby-carl-gustaf.pdf.

Casey, R.D., 1962. Science will "go to people" at World's Fair. Minneapolis Tribune.

Cities under glass: A. Spilhaus's scheme for solving the problems of urban sprawl. 1968. Newsweek. January 8.

Cohn, Victor, 1957. 'U' dean says Russ violated spirit of plan. Minneapolis Tribune. October 5.

Cohn, Victor, 1959. What the bottom of the ocean can tell us. Minneapolis Tribune. June 28.

Cohn, Victor, 1962. I think about the future. Minneapolis Tribune.

Couper, B.K., LaFond, E.C., 1970. Mechanical Bathythermograph: An Historic Review. Advances in Instrumentation 25(3): 735-770.

Court Treatt, Major Chaplin, Court Treatt, Stella, 1926. Cape to Cairo film. www.crossley-motors.org.uk/history/1920/court_treatt/cape _cairo_index.html.

Court Treatt, Stella, 1927. Cape to Cairo. Harrap, London.

Cousteau, Jacques, 1960. The Twentieth Century 'The Power of the Sea: Part 1, TV documentary.

Cronkite, Walter, 1985. Episode 6, Walter Cronkite's Universe.

Death of Dr. Nellie Spilhaus. 1972. Newspaper clipping, South Africa (source unknown). December.

Doel, Ronald, 1989. Interview of Athelstan Spilhaus by Ronald Doel on November 10, 1989. Niels Bohr Library and Archives, American Institute of Physics, College Park, MD. www.aip.org/history -programs/niels-bohr-library/oral-histories/5059.

Donohue, A., 1998. Former dean served 3 presidents, launched skyway system, Minnesota Daily. April 1.

Draper, C.S., Spilhaus, A.F., 1934. Power supplies for suction-driven gyroscopic aircraft instruments. Transactions of the American Society of Mechanical Engineers 56: 289-294.

Dr. Athelstan Spilhaus will wed Mrs. Griffin. 1964. New York Times. January 29.

Educator in orbit. 1959. Time. August 3.

Federal Bureau of Investigation, 1966. Files on Athelstan Spilhaus. Available through the Dolph Briscoe Center for American History, University of Texas at Austin.

Findlay, John, circa 2007. Lesson twenty-five: The impact of the Cold War on Washington: The 1962 Seattle World's Fair, HSTAA 432: History of Washington State and the Pacific Northwest, Center for the Study of the Pacific Northwest, University of Washington. www.washington.edu/uwired/outreach/cspn/Website/Classroom% 20Materials/Pacific%20Northwest%20History/Lessons/Lessons% 2025/25.html.

Flanagan, B., circa 1958. Moon's hidden face moves dean to poetry. Minneapolis Star.

Foster, A.E., 2000. Aeronautical Science 101: The Development of Engineering Science in Aeronautical Engineering Education at the University of Minnesota. Master's thesis, University of Minnesota Twin Cities.

Graham, David, 1984. Dr. Athelstan Spilhaus: Ocean community's Michelangelo. Sea Technology 55.

Graham, David, 1992. Spilhaus revisited: An ocean community's conscience. Sea Technology 43-45.

Graham, David, 1993. Spilhaus: Liquid assets and other "points of light." Sea Technology 60-61.

Gray, James. 1958. Open Wide the Doors. Putnam, New York.

Hutchinson, D., 1990. An 'old shoe' among geniuses: Athelstan Spilhaus. Fauquier 3(4): 5-10.

Knauss, John, 1966. Introduction and Summary. Proceedings of the National Conference on the Concept of a Sea-Grant University, 1. University of Rhode Island, Newport.

Lewis, W., et al. (Eds.), 1954. The Nation Looks at its Resources: Report of the Mid-Century Conference on Resources for the Future.

Livezey, E.T., 1981. Athelstan Spilhaus. The Christian Science Monitor. January 29.

McAndrew, 1st Lt. James, 1995. Report on Project MOGUL, Synopsis of Balloon Research Findings, USAFR. muller.lbl.gov/teaching/physics10/Roswell/USMogulReport.html.

McLain, Clifford, 1998. Eulogy for Athelstan Spilhaus. Recording. Minnesota Sea Grant archives.

Miloy, John, 1983. Creating the College of the Sea: The Origin of the Sea Grant Program, Marine Information Service, Texas A & M University, College Station.

Minnesota Experimental City Authority, 1963–1973. Records. 10.5 cubic feet of material. Minnesota Historical Society, St. Paul.

Minnesota Experimental City papers (N 71). No date. Northwest Architectural Archives. University of Minnesota Libraries.

Misa, Thomas, Seidel, Robert, 2010. IT 75: College of Science and Engineering, Charles Babbage Institute, University of Minnesota Twin Cities.

Mrs. Spilhaus granted divorce. 1964. Minneapolis Star. Undated clipping, circa January.

National Sea Grant College Program Act. 1966. Public Law 89-688, 80 Stat. 998. Enacted by the United States Congress.

The newest new town. 1973. Time. February 26.

Nierenberg, W.A., 2000. Athelstan Spilhaus. Proceedings of the American Philosophical Society 144(3): 343-347.

Ninety-Third Annual Meeting of the American Fisheries Society. 1964. Transactions of the American Fisheries Society 93(1): 109-125.

O'Connor, Louise, 1990a. Cape to Cairo video. 28:02 minutes. www.seagrant.umn.edu/about/spilhaus.

O'Connor, Louise, 1990b. Unpublished oral transcripts of interviews with Dr. Spilhaus. Available through the Dolph Briscoe Center for American History, University of Texas at Austin.

Registers heat and humidity. 1935. Popular Science. June, p. 33.

Ryan, P., 1987. Athelstan Spilhaus: Renaissance man. Oceanus 30(4): 99-104.

Rydell, R.W., et al., 2000. Fair America. Smithsonian Books, Washington, DC.

Scholar's Walk: Who's on the Wall. No date. University of Minnesota. www.scholarswalk.umn.edu/discovery/wall_names.html.

Sea Grant Colleges Hearings before the Subcommittee on Sea Grant Colleges, US Senate, 89th Congress, 1966. Transcript. May 2-5. archive.org/stream/seagrantcolleges00unit/seagrantcolleges00unit _djvu.txt.

Solis-Cohen, L., Solis-Cohen, S., 1993. Mechanical toys are being moved from a world-class collection. Philadelphia Inquirer. July 2.

Spilhaus quits congressional race. 1970. Palm Beach Post. July 16.

Spilhaus: "U" has become great mediocrity. 1967. Minneapolis Star. September 25.

Trunt, Leo, 1998. Boydville becomes Swatara: Excerpt from Beyond the Circle, A Guide to Minnesota Communities. www.lakesnwoods.com/ SwataraHistory.htm.

Tryk, Sheila. 1970. Spilhaus samples school luncheon. Palm Beach Post. October 14.

U Dean Spilhaus will be "gadfly." 1966. St. Paul Pioneer Press. June 12.

Untitled film about Sea Grant, 1990. Available through Minnesota Sea Grant archives.

Vadus, Joseph, 1992. Marine Technological Society meeting recording. Archived at Minnesota Sea Grant, Duluth.

Vadus, Joseph, 1998. Dr. Athelstan Frederick Spilhaus: Eulogy. Minnesota Sea Grant archives.

The Wanderer, circa 1927. The sand racer. Cape Town newspaper, Cape Town, South Africa.

The Wanderer, circa 1960. Space boffin back in his home town. Talk at the Tavern of the Seas. Cape Town newspaper, Cape Town, South Africa.

Weir, Gary, 2001. An Ocean in Common: American Naval Officers, Scientists, and the Ocean Environment. Williams-Ford Texas A & M University Military History Series, College Station.

Weir, Gary, 2004. Fashioning Naval Oceanography: Columbus O'Donnell Iselin and American Preparation for War, 1940–1941. In: Rozwadowski, H.M., Van Keuren, D.K. (Eds.), The Machine in Neptune's Garden: Historical Perspectives on Technology and the Marine Environment. Science History Publications, Sagamore Beach, MA.

Wildermuth, Todd, 2008. Yesterday's City of Tomorrow: The Minnesota Experimental City and Green Urbanism. Dissertation. Department of

Natural Resource and Environmental Science, University of Illinois, Urbana-Champaign.

Woods Hole Oceanographic Institution, 1998. In Memoriam: Athelstan Fredrick Spilhaus. April 1.

Zhuikov, M., 1998. Bag o' lamprey. The Seiche Newsletter. Minnesota Sea Grant, Duluth.

INDEX

Page numbers in boldface (**21**) represent photographs and images.

About the Author

When Sharon Moen was approached about writing this biography, she only had the vaguest of notions that Spilhaus was an oceanographer who somehow became misplaced in Minnesota and invented the Sea Grant program. Over the seven years that it took to bring *With Tomorrow in Mind* to press, she became keenly aware of what many others grasped before and what a generation could be poised to forget: Spilhaus was the "ocean community's Michelangelo."

Photo by John Steffl

Moen has a bachelor's of science in biology from Pennsylvania State University and a master's of science in ecology, evolution, and behavior from the University of Minnesota. Well into her second decade with Minnesota Sea Grant, Moen believes, like Spilhaus, in pursuing diverse interests. When she is not at her desk, she can be found at the potter's wheel, larking about outdoors (preferably in a canoe), or standing motionless, transfixed by birds.